THE APPLE OF HIS EYE

This book is dedicated, with love, to my mother and father, and also to Matt, Joe, David and Katy, each one definitely the apple of my eye (whatever I may have called them at times!)

THE APPLE OF HIS EYE

BRIDGET PLASS

The Bible Reading Fellowship
OPENING THE BIBLE

Text copyright © Bridget Plass 1996

The author asserts the moral right
to be identified as the author of this work

Published by
The Bible Reading Fellowship
First Floor, Elsfield Hall
15–17 Elsfield Way,
Oxford OX2 8FG
ISBN 1 84101 088 X

First edition 1996
This edition 1999
10 9 8 7 6 5 4 3 2 1

Acknowledgments
Unless otherwise indicated, scripture quotations are taken from the Good News Bible
published by The Bible Societies/HarperCollins Publishers Ltd, UK © American Bible
Society 1966, 1971, 1976, 1992, used with permission.

Scripture quotations taken from the Holy Bible, New International Version, copyright
© 1973, 1978, 1984 by International Bible Society. Used by permission of Hodder &
Stoughton Limited. All rights reserved. 'NIV' is a registered trademark of International
Bible Society. UK trademark number 1448790.

A catalogue record for this book is available from the British Library

Printed and bound in Great Britain by Omnia Books Ltd, Glasgow

CONTENTS

The beautiful picture on the cover of *The Apple of His Eye* is called 'The Prodigal Son'. A mosaic by the late Hildegart Nicholas, and made up of 10,000 pieces, it is in the Chapel of The Royal Bournemouth Hospital. We are very grateful to them for giving us permission to use it.

We had looked at literally hundreds of pictures to find one for the cover of Bridget Plass's delightful and original book, but not one of them fitted. Then, when I was seeing Bishop Richard Harries about something entirely different, and because I knew how much he knows about art, I asked him if he could help. He thought for a moment, and then said: 'There's a mosaic by Hildegart Nicholas. We've got a copy of it, so I'll go and fetch it.'

We are immensely grateful for this suggestion, and to Richard and Jo Harries for lending us their photograph to work from. It is very precious to them, because it was signed by Hildegart Nicholas. We also want to thank her husband, Sir Barry Nicholas, for agreeing to let us use the picture.

Shelagh Brown
Bible Reading Fellowship

FOREWORD

Before you get a chance to look at the first page *The Apple Of His Eye*—my first book—I want to say that I agreed to write it with some trepidation. I am all too aware that I am not a professional writer—and all too aware that my husband Adrian is! However, I have for years enjoyed communicating the Bible in the form of preaching and Bible teaching and as Adrian and I travel further and further around the world it never fails to amaze me that so many people in the Church seem to have missed out on the best truth of all. The truth that they really, really are God's children and that he delights in them. Not in some airy-fairy sort of way, not in an arms-length formal handshaking sort of way, but in the extravagantly over-the-top way that we all want to be loved by our parents and, if we have them, our children want to be loved by us.

As you read this book, I'd like you to join me as I explore some aspects of this love, especially in the light of what Jesus told us about his Father. We will be looking at some things that took place during the last few weeks of Jesus' life here on earth, and at God's loving purpose in the lives of a few of his children. I also hope you will join me in walking with Jesus himself as he resolutely turned his face towards Jerusalem and his death.

This will be a very personal interpretation. I am not, by any stretch of the imagination, a biblical scholar. But my hope is that through these studies you will catch a glimpse of what it means to be the apple of God's eye.

Bridget Plass

JESUS SAYS :- "OH o DON'T FORGET."
LAST MIN. MESSAGES.
REMEMBER GOD WANTS TO BE OUR FATHER.
COURAGE TO GET UP IN THE MORNING.
ANY COMPLAINTS ABOUT THIS NODAR - REFER TO
DON'T LIKE OURSELVES. BUILDS RELATIONSHIP WITH GOD. HIS MAKER.
LOVE.
GOD SO PLEASED TO SEE US WAITING FOR HIM TO
BE ABLE TO GO TO HVY.

SECTION 1

'OH, AND BEFORE I GO...'

You know how just before you are going away you keep thinking of urgent messages that you want to leave behind? 'Oh, and don't forget to...' type messages for the people who will be left behind at home or at work. And you keep repeating them to yourself because your mind is so distracted? And every time you think of something it feels so vitally important you just have to say it again?

Well, this is how it seems to have been with Jesus during the period before he allowed himself to be taken to his death. But his urgent messages were not about the milkman or the taxman. They were all about God. 'Did I tell you he's your Father?... Oh and don't forget he wants you to call him Father... You must remember he loves you like a father... He loves you like I do... When you've seen me you've seen the Father... Oh and don't forget he...'

Did you know John records the word 'Father' thirty-nine times in chapters 14 to 17 of his account of the last weeks of the life of Jesus?

Because of Jesus' sense of urgency during this emotionally charged period I thought we would begin these studies by concentrating on a few of the startling facts about God our Father that his children have discovered about him throughout the Bible.

REFER DIRECTLY TO MAKER

You created every part of me;
You put me together in my mother's womb.
I praise you because you are to be feared;
all you do is strange and wonderful.
I know it with all my heart.
When my bones were being formed,
Carefully put together in my mother's womb,
when I was growing there in secret,
you knew that I was there—
you saw me before I was born.

I don't know if you've been able to see a photo of an ultrasound scan showing the human foetus at an early stage. I think it's one of the most marvellous things I have ever seen. A tiny knobbly lump holding all the intricate patterns of God's little masterpiece. Biology textbooks used in schools now all contain pictures of the developing embryo. My favourite is a photograph taken at eighteen weeks showing a minuscule thumb being sucked. Have you seen it? It is quite beautiful and seems full of mysteries. What colour are those eyes, hooded at present by a delicate pink film? Is it a boy or a girl? Will it have big feet like Grandma, or Great-Uncle's nose?

Having had four children whose personalities are all quite individual, I'm particularly intrigued by another unknown quality. What personality will it have, Martha or Mary? Will it have a volcanic temper? What will make it laugh? How will it instinctively handle grief? What will be its thorn in the flesh and its particular talent?

God knows. Literally! He knows every single thing about this being-to-be and, we are told, loves it even more than any mother can.

I couldn't begin to explain why some of these tiny miracles carry future pain within them even at this stage, some physical or mental disablement that will make their lives so much more difficult than it is for most of us.

The only thing I can confidently pass on is something that a friend told me. Her name is Hilary McDowell, and she was born with a huge personality but also multiple injuries to her minuscule body. It was the determination, love and faith of her family which helped her develop the first and overcome the second sufficiently to lead a full life.

We met at Carberry House, a Christian conference and holiday centre in Scotland. In between her performance poetry evening, her dance workshops for teenagers and her counselling in her role as deaconess we found lots of time for 'a bit of wee crack'. (This by the way was a little chat! Hilary comes from Belfast.)

She told me how sometimes it is very, very hard to get up in the morning. Looking forward to a day of painful physical struggle takes a daily dose of courage which occasionally deserts her at seven in the morning. On those occasions she says she needs to look at the little poem she has stuck above the mirror in her bedroom. It is the shortest poem she has written and is included in her fascinating first book, *Some Day I'm Going To Fly*. This is what it says:

'Any complaints about this model refer directly to maker!'

That's it. A tiny statement containing the essence of the mystery of why we are as we are. As simple yet intricate as the embryo.

So many of us just don't like ourselves. We look in the mirror and we don't like what we see or what we know is inside. It is hampering our happiness, ruining our relationship with God, turning up like the proverbial bad penny to prevent us from marching forward. So tell God about it. Tell him how you can't cope today, how fed up and unhappy you are. Take your complaints to him. He made you and he alone will be able to answer your questions. And, let's face it, he has loved you longest!

PRAYER

Dear Father,

    Here I am, your child, your grown-up baby. Sometimes I don't like myself very much, sometimes I can't cope. Sometimes I want to give up. Sometimes getting up in the morning and facing the day is almost too hard to do. Sometimes I hate you for not sorting it out, for allowing the things that have made me as I am. Love me through it all, my dear Father, and help me to see myself as you see me.

I'M HERE, GOD!

PSALM 17:6–9 (NIV)

I call on you, O God, for you will answer me;
give ear to me and hear my prayer.
Show the wonder of your great love,
you who save by your right hand
those who take refuge in you from their foes.
Keep me as the apple of your eye;
hide me in the shadow of your wings
from the wicked who assail me,
from my mortal enemies who surround me.

I had had a really depressed phone call from Adrian. He had been speaking for the first time in Germany, with the aid of a translator, and it had been very difficult. Although the tour had gone well, and despite the tremendous hospitality, he had felt very lonely, as he spoke no German at all. He was longing to come home. So the children and I decided to give him a surprise and go and meet him off his plane the next day.

Now trying to give Adrian this sort of surprise is never easy, as he is notoriously disorganized (as I am) and it turned out that he had got the time of the arrival of his flight wrong by several hours. But of course we didn't know that and, having got up at the crack of dawn, we spent the best part of the day at Heathrow with very little money and increasingly fraying tempers. In fact by the time the news that his plane had landed came up on the screen we were in a bad way!

The two middle boys, having sparred all afternoon, had fallen out with a vengeance and because the arrivals lounge at Heathrow hardly seemed a suitable venue for a shirt-ripping war I had got very very cross with them both. And knowing how carried away I can get I probably told them they had let down not only their entire family, but also their queen, their country, and indeed the whole human race. I don't exactly recall what I said. But I do remember the pall of shame which reduced them to a sad snuffling huddle and my own feelings of failure.

It was therefore quite a surprise to me to watch them both quite individually choose a spot right in the front of the crowd when they saw the words 'baggage in hall' come up on the monitor screen. I knew they were feeling very bad about themselves and would not have been surprised if they had skulked at the back. Then Adrian came round the corner, and I watched his tired eyes light up as he saw his sons waiting for him. In that split second I learnt something very important.

I meet so many Christians who are living their lives in a sort of 'at-the-back skulk', and because they feel so ashamed of something they have done they have convinced themselves that God would not particularly want to see them. I also meet people all the time who find it difficult to pray because their sense of self-worth is so low that they don't really think he would want to hear from them.

Watching Adrian hugging his two grubby sons together, I knew.

The reason why we, the inadequate ones, should feel confident enough to metaphorically stand at the front of the crowd and shout 'I'm here, God! Look over here, it's me!' is not because of what we are or how well we are behaving. It is quite simply because we are the apple of his eye and the sight of us can't help but give him joy—because he is crackers about us.

Dear Father,

Are we really that special to you? Can it really be true that whatever we may do nothing can separate us from your love? Help us to believe it. Help us to stand straight and tall and confident in your love.

HEAVENLY GLUE

JEREMIAH 18:1−6 (NIV)

This is the word that came to Jeremiah from the Lord: 'Go down to the potter's house and there I will give you my message.'

So I went down to the potter's house and I saw him working at the wheel. But the pot he was shaping from the clay was marred in his hands; so the potter formed it into another pot, shaping it as seemed best to him.

Then the word of the Lord came to me: 'O house of Israel, can I not do with you as this potter does?' declares the Lord. 'Like clay in the hand of the potter, so are you in my hand, O house of Israel.'

One of our best friends locally is a builder and decorator who also runs a small but lively church fellowship. This combination leads him into dealing with very diverse situations so we were somewhat intrigued when his small son solemnly announced one day, 'I know what my Dad does.'

'Oh do you! What does he do then?' Adrian asked.

'He fills in cracks' Tom replied with considerable pride.

I had to work overtime to suppress my laughter. Knowing the wide variety of skills our friend needs to carry out his slightly unusual role we felt his son had hardly done him justice. Fortunately his dad found it funny too, his only worry being whether his son had been made to look silly when he told us.

This passage about the potter has caused me a lot of problems over the years. I have always had difficulty with the idea of being smashed and remoulded, perhaps because I have felt so strongly that my pot is such a mess that that would be the only option for it! Consequently I have wasted a lot of time trying to bash myself into shape on the quiet just in order to avoid the humiliation of God having to do it.

I have also had a fear that God wants us all to be exactly the same. This has caused me to panic on many occasions. The idea of a line of pretty, perfect, identical little pots in which I would somehow be the odd one out is not an unfamiliar one to me. Some church teaching has made me feel like that.

Three things have helped me greatly in my understanding of what this image means. They might just help you.

One was the above conversation. The more I thought about it the more I felt it to be a remarkable parable of the way God has decided to be with us. He is the master potter and each of us is just a thimble of his creation. Yet our experience of him is of someone who is not offended by our limited understanding of how truly awesome he is. He can take it because he is huge and completely in control, not some temperamental prima donna who will hurl us to the wall because we have got dirty or misshapen through our contact with the world and somehow let his image down. The problem is that the dirtier we get the more distorted our image of him will be, and the less likely we will be to trust him with the necessary repairs.

The second is the information that Jesus is continually trying to communicate to his followers about the fatherhood of God. God is more likely, then—after maybe quite a showdown—to lick the corner of a father-sized handkerchief and scrub off the grime once we have said sorry for any damage and filth we have deliberately inflicted on ourselves. Incidentally Jesus also makes it very clear that damage done to one of his new unsullied pots by anyone else makes God very very angry.

The third thing that helped me greatly was hearing someone say that the potter never throws away the clay. When I heard that I recognized my deepest fear has been that I could be rejected completely by the Master Potter. Thrown away. Deemed beyond repair. I suspect I am not the first person to have felt like that.

Well, I felt such a surge of excitement and joy on realizing the truth contained in that book that I found myself wanting to perform one of those ludicrously extravagant punches in the air that accompany the scoring of a goal in football. Yes!!

Of course! He's crazy about the clay! He chose it. He made us. Every bit. He will never smash us to the point of non-identity. Only knead us into shape like an expert physiotherapist and clean us so that our intended individual colouring will be seen more clearly.

We haven't come off some assembly line supervised by bored workers longing for their next tea break. Each one of us has been individually designed with passion and love and is intended to be unique. Every tiny chip that appears on the surface of our special glaze saddens our creator because his concern for us is that we should feel beautiful and useful.

But he's been using chipped pots to do useful things for him ever since the fall. They're the only ones he has to work with. Isaac, Jacob, Moses, Gideon, David, Matthew, Peter, Paul, to name just a few. He has always seemed quite prepared to pour the heavenly glue of his love and support into any amount of cracks if his children have been prepared to trust him.

Bearing all this in mind, and wanting to impress you with my mature and balanced attitude to my new-found confidence, all I can say is that

I'm a little teapot,
Short and stout,
Here's my handle,
Here's my spout.
When the kettle's boiling
You can pour me...

Well, perhaps not! I'll just go back to punching the air! Why don't you join me? Yes!!

Here we are, Lord.

A pile of chipped, grubby pots. We want to be useful again. We want to be beautiful in your eyes. Take us in your expert hands, dear Father, and do whatever needs doing in order for that to be so. We could all do with some heavenly glue! Thank you for loving us unconditionally. Thank you for making us exactly as you wanted us to be. Please forgive us for any damage we have done to ourselves and others and help us to be willing to begin the process of forgiving those who have deliberately violated us.

Here we are, Lord. Please begin mending us— however long it takes. Amen.

GOD OUR STRENGTH

PSALM 73:21–26

When my thoughts were bitter and my feelings were hurt,
I was as stupid as an animal;
I did not understand you.
Yet I always stay close to you
and you hold me by the hand.
You guide me with your instruction
and at the end you will receive me with honour.
What else have I in heaven but you?
Since I have you, what else could I want on earth?
My mind and my body may grow weak,
but God is my strength;
he is all I ever need.

I am about to tell you something about myself that won't impress you much. It's rather good about God, though! It was about a year after God had pulled my husband through a breakdown, stood him up, dusted him down and given him a job to do. At first I had been just so thrilled to see Adrian regaining confidence, getting to know his spiritual Father and proving rather useful in the role God had chosen for him. It was particularly exciting to see how what he was writing was having such a freeing effect on those who read his books.

Gradually, however, I found that I was not actually feeling as happy as all that. Strong feelings of hurt and confusion began to dominate my life. Not being someone brimming over with confidence I had been badly bashed by some of the side effects of

Adrian's illness—the money worries, the insecurity, the isolation and loneliness—but all the way through I had felt tremendous confidence that God would sort it out for us. Now he had but there were new costs involved. I had thought God would put our lives back to how they had been before the crack-up. He hadn't!

It felt as though Adrian's life had begun at 37¾ and our life together with all its recent intensity didn't exist. He had become overnight that most extraordinary phenomenon, a 'famous Christian', and it felt as though he was public property! He was frequently away from home, and I discovered I was in fact very fed up with God and even jealous of Adrian.

'You don't actually care one hoot about me do you?' I'd rage at God. 'All you care about is Adrian. You just wanted to get Adrian well so he could work for you. What about me? Don't you care? Don't you love me at all?'

Looking back I can see that a lot of it was a natural reaction to a long period of having to be strong. But at the time it was awful. Apart from all this ghastly hurt, I felt so guilty, especially when I began to take it out on Adrian. All day when I knew he was going away I'd really try to be a good Christian wife—and then just as he was going out of the door my good resolve would disintegrate and I'd hear myself yelling like the proverbial fishwife.

Poor Adrian frequently had to stand in front of hundreds of people telling them how much God loved them and wanted to set them free—with my cruel words ringing in his ears.

At last I decided that I must do something or I would destroy all the healing that had taken place in my husband and endanger the work God had given him. I decided to get away for a few days to 'sort out my life'.

I travelled to Scargill House in Yorkshire, armed with questions and arguments to put to God, and I think I fully intended to come home having decided on some sort of job that would fulfil me and make me mind less about Adrian's new lifestyle.

When I got there an extraordinary thing happened. It was as though suddenly I could see clearly again after a long period of blindness. Absolutely no insights about my life took place at all!

They seemed quite irrelevant. All I could think about was Jesus. It was as if he held me by the hand for the whole of the three days and I experienced a senseless joy that you only have when you first fall in love.

Of course there were practical areas of our lives which we had to sort out. But at last I knew that I was going to be able to look at them realistically and face the fact that our lives would never be as they had been before, because I had been reminded that God is my strength and he is all I ever need.

PRAYER

Dear Father,

Sometimes we can end up so far away from you, blinded by our anger, stupefied by our hurt. If we have got confused, take control of our lives, we beg you, Father. If we have got lost, come and find us and bring us home. We miss you. We want to see you again. Come soon.

WIDE, LONG, HIGH AND DEEP

EPHESIANS 3:17-21 (NIV)

*[I pray] that Christ will dwell in your hearts through faith.
And I pray that you, being rooted and established in love,
may have power, together with all the saints, to grasp how
wide and long and high and deep is the love of Christ, and
to know this love that surpasses knowledge—that you may
be filled to the measure of all the fullness of God.*

*Now to him who is able to do immeasurably more than
all we ask or imagine, according to his power that is at
work within us, to him be glory in the church and in
Christ Jesus throughout all generations, for ever and ever!
Amen.*

I was still in Scargill and the last day of my mini-retreat had
arrived. I woke early to the strange sound of nothingness and
peering through the misted window realized that it had been
snowing heavily during the night.

Stunningly lovely as the countryside looked I was worried.
How would we all get out? The conference centre was surrounded
by tiny lanes which must already be inches deep in snow.
Hurrying downstairs I found several people already packed and
preparing to go. 'I've just been listening to the local news,' one of
the leaders announced. 'The forecast for later on in the day is
pretty dire but the local roads are still passable. So it's really a
choice of going now or being prepared for being snowed up here
for a few days.'

If the whole family had been with me I think I would have

decided to stay. Snowballing and sledging in the Yorkshire Fells would have been heavenly. But they weren't. They were 300 miles away in Hailsham and I was missing them like mad. I ran upstairs, grabbed my case, hurried down, hugged and thanked and skidded my way to the car.

The first twenty miles were very nasty but eventually I made it to the motorway. Relaxing, I turned on the car radio. The news was worse than I'd thought possible. Apparently roads all the way across the country were in chaos. Accidents were becoming commonplace and people were being firmly advised only to venture out if their journey was absolutely vital. Conditions seemed to be getting more treacherous every minute.

The snow was coming down thickly and visibility was getting worse. So was the news. Information was coming in all the time of crashes and breakdowns, along with warnings to stay in your car at all costs and advice not to venture out without defroster, bin bag, thermos and torch. I had none of those things and was very aware that I had been silly to attempt the journey.

All the euphoria that I had experienced over the last few days had gone and I felt frightened and incredibly vulnerable. So much for my renewed closeness with God. So much for feeling that he really did care deeply about me after all. Visibility became even worse as tears began to pour down my face. I was 200 miles away from home, freezing cold and what was more it was beginning to get dark.

At that moment my car gave a groan and shuddered to almost a halt. I was aware of someone swerving to avoid me. Now I was slithering at two miles an hour, sure that any minute I would be hit. In front of me I could just make out a sign indicating a turning to the left and, feeling that anything would be better than breaking down on the motorway, I wobbled the car onto a side road. I could see nothing at all. 'My lights must have gone down,' I thought and immediately, with a horrifying bang, the car stopped completely.

I sat there in the pitch darkness in my dead car and cried out to God in desperation. Then I opened my eyes. There to the left of me, its blurry lights just visible through the driving snow, was a café and travel lodge!

Now I have heard of people who believe that God runs ahead of them every time they go to the supermarket just to reserve a parking space for them—and quite honestly I don't have a lot of time for the idea that Christians should expect continual privileges. But I do believe that on that night God arranged exactly when and where my car broke down. That night, having phoned both home and the AA, I sat warm and safe in a bed with a cup of tea, watching horrendous television news pictures of abandoned cars on motorways up and down the country.

I will never forget the sense I had of my heavenly Father very close to me saying, 'I had to prove to you somehow how wide, long, high and deep my love is for you, you stubborn woman!'

I wonder how he'll show you!

PRAYER

Dear Father,

We so want to feel close to you. Help us to open ourselves to the possibility that you will meet us and that you really do want us to experience the depth of love that Paul is talking about here.

BREAK OUT THE SMARTIES!

Lord, you have examined me and you know me.
You know everything I do;
from far away you understand all my thoughts.
You see me whether I am working or resting;
you know all my actions.
Even before I speak,
you already know what I will say.
You are all round me on every side;
you protect me with your power.
Your knowledge of me is too deep;
it is beyond my understanding.

The tremendous good news contained in this psalm was highlighted for me by something that happened yesterday. It was at a club which the joint churches in our town hold for local children, many of whom come from very difficult backgrounds.

It had been an exhausting but exciting morning and I had been particularly pleased with the behaviour of one small toughy. When he started he had been impossible to reach and had reacted aggressively to just about everything. Gradually, over a period of about two years, his suspicions had eased to the point that he even allowed a little teasing and physical contact. Today he had been lovely and I wanted to show him how pleased I was.

'Patrick, I'm really proud of you. Here's a special secret prize for trying so hard,' I whispered, surreptitiously opening the 'prize box', and sliding a tube of Smarties into his hand. 'Fanks, Miss,' he beamed, and ran off, shovelling handfuls of sweets into his mouth as he went. Putting the lid back on the box, I placed it on the table and went off to join in with the sorting out of chaos, replacing of felt-tip pen lids and scraping glue off tables that inevitably accompanied the close of a meeting. I felt really happy.

Ten minutes later my friend Phillippa put something into my hand. It was an identical, unopened tube of Smarties.

'I saw Patrick pinch it from the prize box on the way out,' she said, smiling, 'so I thought I'd better tackle him.'

'Oh no,' I groaned, 'and I'd only just given him exactly the same thing as a prize for being so *good* today!'

'Well,' she laughed, 'look at it this way, six months ago he would have denied he took them and probably kicked me in the shins for insulting him!'

God knows exactly where we all start our Christian walk. He knows exactly why we are as we are and what are our weaknesses, and it could well be that all heaven rejoiced that morning because Phillippa didn't have her shins kicked!

It's easy to see God's loving forgiveness and encouragement with regard to little Patrick. But how about yourself? I wonder what we may have done recently that has made heaven rejoice? What small step we have made towards depending more on him? What temptation we have resisted? What kind thought we have had? It may not seem much to us—and I know my own progress seems agonizingly slow, but to a God who knows us inside out it may have brought a smile and even heaven's equivalent to a hug and a tube of Smarties!

PRAYER

Dear Father,

Thank heavens(!) you know everything about us. You see exactly where we began, what the obstacles are to our progress and you know exactly where you would expect us to be right now. Give us strength to

pick ourselves up when we fail and carry on, knowing that you will be so pleased to see every little step of progress in our stumbling walk towards you.

WHOSE SIDE IS GOD ON?

JONAH 3:1 – 6, 10; 4:1 – 2

Once again the Lord spoke to Jonah. He said, 'Go to Nineveh, that great city, and proclaim to the people the message I have given you.' So Jonah obeyed the Lord and went to Nineveh, a city so large that it took three days to walk through it. Jonah started through the city, and after walking a whole day, he proclaimed, 'In forty days Nineveh will be destroyed.'

The people of Nineveh believed God's message. So they decided that everyone should fast, and all the people from the greatest to the least, put on sackcloth to show that they had repented... God saw what they did; he saw that they had given up their wicked behaviour. So he changed his mind and did not punish them as he had said he would.

Jonah was very unhappy about this and became angry. So he prayed, 'Lord, didn't I say before I left home that this is just what you would do? That's why I did my best to run away to Spain! I knew that you are a loving and merciful God, always patient, always kind, and always ready to change your mind and not punish.'

This story of Jonah contains some wonderful news. Not the fact that if we choose to disobey God there is a possibility that he will arrange for us to be swallowed by a very large fish, but the recorded reason for Jonah's disobedience. He didn't want to tell the citizens of Nineveh that God was angry with their behaviour because he knew without a shadow of doubt that if they said they were sorry God would forgive them.

Jonah knew God. He saw his readiness to forgive as infuriating weakness until God pointed out to him, through the picture of the vine, that the reason he would try again and again to give the people of Nineveh chances to repent was that he had watched their growing up and cared deeply for each one.

Several years ago I came across an example of the same unequivocal sureness about what God would do. We have a friend who grew up in a series of child care establishments. She became increasingly disturbed by the process until at eighteen she was dumped into bed-and-breakfast land, armed with tranquillizers and a severe lack of self-confidence, to fend for herself.

At that stage in her life she was in a terrible mess and made a series of unhappy relationships. She knew we worried about her and phoned frequently to keep us posted about her struggles. At one stage she was living with a man who had left his wife and we knew she was hoping against hope that this time the relationship could lead to marriage.

Very late one night she phoned to tell us, amid many tears, that he was thinking of going back to his wife. Of course we both felt acutely sorry for her and I finished our long chat by saying, 'Before I go to bed I'll pray for you both.'

"'Ere, don't do that, Bridget,' came the scandalized reply. 'You know 'ose side he'll b... well be on!'

Her instinctive response revealed more faith and confidence in the reality and righteousness of God than many sermons I have heard before or since. She and Jonah had a lot in common. Neither wanted God to intervene because they were sure they knew whose side he would be on.

Do I have that confidence? I find that as I grow older I am less sure than I used to be about exactly how I think God will behave in specific situations but increasingly confident that whatever he does will be right. In fact the more I get to know just a fraction of his heart the more I feel able to agree with what Dame Julian of Norwich said: 'All will be well and all manner of things will be well.'

PRAYER

Dear Father,

Thank you for the story of Jonah. What mind-blowing stuff. We want to get to know you like Jonah did. We want to trust deep inside that you will always do what is just and fair. Help us.

THE OFFER OF SAFETY

ZECHARIAH 8:4 – 5 (NIV)

This is what the Lord Almighty says: 'Once again men and women of ripe old age will sit in the streets of Jerusalem, each with cane in hand because of his age. The city streets will be filled with boys and girls playing there.'

When I came across these verses recently I felt as if I had found an answer to something that has been troubling me for so long. Why don't we feel the same urgency that Jesus felt to tell the world about our Father God? Of course some of the reasons are obvious: laziness, fear, indifference... but I think one of the most crucial reasons is that deep down we don't think God has got anything to offer that the world seems to want. We think our message is too unworldly for our world.

When we first went to Australia we attended a marvellous conference organized by the Uniting Church. They had chosen for their title 'This Is The Life' and I remember, on the day we arrived, being told the reason for their choice. It was explained to us that Australians would only be attracted by a positive lifestyle message because of the deep-seated self-made philosophy which had served them so well. The gospel with its message of self-sacrifice was not apparently much of a winner here.

When we returned two years later and got to meet many Australians over a far wider area we appreciated the reasons for their choice of title. But we also realized that on a deeper level many were desperate to be allowed to be vulnerable and to admit to feelings of fear and insecurity. There were more tears shed during that tour than on any other and many of them by men who were discovering that what God was offering them was what they had always really wanted.

For me that was the key to understanding what God had said to Zechariah, because I realized that God wants for us is what we—and I mean the whole world—most want for ourselves. Security. A world where our old people and our children can walk and play safely in our streets.

I was standing in our local children's playground watching with pretend gasps of horror my friend's small boy attempting to swing hand over hand along a high brightly coloured bar. 'At least he can't hurt himself,' I whispered. 'This new surface is brilliant, he'll practically bounce.' I turned to call four-year-old Katy to come off the slide and have a try. There was no one on the slide. Or the swings. Or the roundabout. Three small boys occupied the wooden pirate ship with blood-curdling threats of plank-walking for invaders so I knew she couldn't be there.

Panic doesn't come in slowly. It rushes in and engulfs like a monstrous wave. I began to run round the small fenced area willing her to be tucked behind the wooden bench or under the slide. The spectre all parents fear was filling my mind.

Then I saw her. Dancing and jumping across the recreation field with her hand tucked securely into that of her big brother. She had seen him coming and run to meet him. Nothing to worry about this time—but as I stood there watching her Piglet-like approach a stark truth hit me. The new technologically advanced surfaces have at last made playgrounds safe places for young children to play on. But no caring parent lets their small children out of their sight to play in them. The danger is too great!

Maybe this is a clue as to how to speak more confidently to those who don't want to hear. So very often we hear God described by those who haven't met him as a demanding tyrant or an indifferent judge. Yet here he is acknowledging as vitally important the very thing we all yearn for most.

PRAYER

Dear Father,

Give us the confidence to tell our world about you. Help us to remember that you care deeply about your world and want for every one of your children, young and old, safety and peace. We want to say sorry for all the times when we have missed opportunities to talk about you. And for the times we have misrepresented you in some way and so not given strength to your word. Lastly, Father, as your children, we ask you please to keep our loved ones safe.

BACK TO EDEN?

GENESIS 1:26−31

Then God said, 'And now we will make human beings; they will be like us and resemble us. They will have power over the fish, the birds and all animals, domestic and wild, large and small.' So God created human beings, making them to be like himself. He created them male and female, blessed them and said, 'Have many children so that your descendants will live over all the earth and bring it under their control. I am putting you in charge of the fish, the birds and all the wild animals. I have provided all kinds of grain and all kinds of fruit for you to eat; but for all the wild animals and for all the birds I have provided grass and leafy plants for food'—and it was done. God looked at everything he had made, and he was very pleased.

We spent the summer of '95 working in South Africa. It was a tremendous experience for all of us and we met some fascinating people.

Yuri and his wife, Pippa, ran a small safari lodge on the edge of the Kruger National Park. At the end of our speaking tour we spent three of the most exciting days of our lives there.

None of us will forget the smells and sights of our early morning treks into the bushveld, as we bumped excitedly along in an open-topped jeep. We saw so many wild creatures, sometimes from quite frighteningly close quarters.

One of our most memorable experiences, however, didn't involve elephants or lions. It was a walk along a quiet trail through the area of wilderness right next to the camp. We were with Yuri, who was a trained ecologist, and Dixon, our black South African ranger, who followed closely with a loaded rifle, just in case! Yuri was a veritable mine of local knowledge, continually throwing out nuggets of information as we walked. We learnt more in that hour as we strolled along looking at bushes and insects than I would have imagined possible.

There was the baobab tree that had been formed with a fireproof bark to protect it from the fires which burn the savannah to the ground every year during the hot dry season and provide fertile soil for renewed growth. There were the follow-my-leader troops of ants; a discarded tortoise shell whose pattern revealed the age of its former owner, long dead; twigs which traditionally would have been used as toothbrushes and, from another bush, leaves that were once the only available toilet paper.

We saw termite heaps that, after falling into disuse, become desirable residences for the dwarf mongoose, and tantalizing glimpses of vervet monkeys foraging for berries. Most moving of all were the little piles of bones which denoted the burial sites of the indigenous tribes who had lived there until the scourge of apartheid had forced them to leave.

We were walking in what is thought to be the cradle of humanity, and on that sun-drenched morning it felt like Eden.

This feeling was fuelled by something that Yuri told us. Apparently the ecosystem of this area belies the theory that man is superfluous to the natural world. Anyone who has seen or read *The Jungle Book* knows that even the king of the jungle didn't know the secret of how to make fire and that that was the reason for capturing the man-cub, Mowgli. The savannah has always needed fire in order to prevent excessive bush encroachment and to maintain grass in lush and palatable condition for the many herbivores who provide food for carnivores, and so on along the food chain. People provided the knowledge the savannah needed for survival.

Much of what Yuri was saying was way over my head, but I

felt that we were privy to a very special understanding of the creation story, made even more poignant by his references to a tiny bird called the honeyguide bird, whose sole function throughout living memory has been to tell people where honey can be found. He sits in a tree and calls until a human being hears him. Calling constantly, and flitting from tree to tree, he guides his follower, sometimes for several days, until they reach a place where a hive full of honey awaits them.

In the days when this might have been people's only source of sweetness it is easy to see how important his role must have been. Now he is redundant. The people who belong here have been driven from their territory into the inappropriately named 'homelands', and, even though more than a year has passed since the democratic elections, show little sign of returning. The only occupants of the area are tourists and safari-camp owners, who are far too busy to spend several days seeking sweetness that they can buy in the local supermarket. Now the honeyguide bird faces extinction.

This profoundly sad story seems to offer an insight into the even greater tragedy of original sin. The 'sin chain', almost as old as the world itself, the inevitable, rolling consequence of greed, selfishness and lust for power, has, again and again, disregarded and destroyed the delicate balance that was always supposed to exist between people, God and the natural world.

PRAYER

Dear Father,

We know we can't put the clock back to the time when all your beautiful world was in harmony. All we can do is ask for forgiveness about the way we have treated our part of it. Help us to understand how best we can improve our corner of the universe. And give us courage to stand against those who are trying to destroy the balance further. Amen.

OUR FATHER...

GALATIANS 3:26 — 4:7 (NIV)

You are all sons of God through faith in Christ Jesus, for all of you who were baptised into Christ have clothed yourselves with Christ. There is neither Jew nor Greek, slave nor free, male nor female, for you are all one in Christ Jesus. If you belong to Christ, then you are Abraham's seed, and heirs according to the promise.

What I am saying is that as long as the heir is a child, he is no different from a slave, although he owns the whole estate. He is subject to guardians and trustees until the time set by his father. So also, when we were children, we were in slavery under the basic principles of the world. But when the time had fully come, God sent his Son, born of a woman, born under law, to redeem those under law, that we might receive the full rights of sons. Because you are sons, God sent the Spirit of his Son into our hearts, the Spirit who calls out, 'Abba, Father.' So you are no longer a slave, but a son; and since you are a son, God has made you also an heir.

Having just returned from our last tour, I realize that one of the characteristics of travelling is the way you both lose and acquire things. A pile of underwear left in a hotel drawer, a sweatshirt on a boat, a handbag stolen, while the whole of the southern hemisphere must be littered to a point of ecological disaster with Plass combs and odd socks! Yet our bags get ever heavier. Innumerable mini-shampoos and bath gels, a wonderful gift painstakingly woven by a group of ladies in Queensland, a special bottle of wine from the Barossa valley, a plethora of mini-koalas and kangaroos and keyrings for presents, a hotel towel that got dyed pink by mistake in the guest laundry and decided that it would be an ugly unwanted duckling among the pristine snow-whiteness of its bathroom family... The list seems endless.

Other more interesting things are acquired along the way. Things that help to make the ever heavier case easier to carry. Friendships struck up over periods of twenty-four hours which because of the lack of time delve deeper into one's heart than many acquaintances who one has known for years. Contact with enthusiasts who communicate their involvement with such commitment and joy that their causes are irresistible, such as one of our tour sponsors, World Vision.

But even more than all of this we have acquired a truth that will never leave us. A knowledge of how truly tiny and vulnerable we all are, and how much God has to love and care for us. That may sound trite but everywhere we go we meet people who are struggling with their relationships, health, work; people clinging to each other to prevent themselves being blown over by the tornado of life, people who love and need love, worrying people, people whose hard shell of success has been cracked by God so that his love can flow in; people who have never developed a shell at all. Children. All children. One huge, loving, squabbling, diverse crowd of kids who haven't understood that they don't need to prove anything, to be right, to be first, to be taller or greater, cleverer or more talented because he has fathered us all and, in a way we'll never understand, can hold all of us, wipe all our tears and listen to all our adventures. Our Father, *Abba*, who art in heaven, hallowed be thy name.

PRAYER

Dear Father,

It is so easy for us to look at the differences between us, your children, in a critical way. Help us to understand, just a tiny bit, the mystery of your ability to love all of us with such passion that you gave us your Son to die for us. Help us to stop squabbling; to share what we have and to enjoy each other's special gifts, without feeling jealous. Above all, help us to learn from one another so that our understanding of your greatness can also grow. Amen.

TOO BUSY?

REVELATION 3:14-20

'This is the message from the Amen, the faithful and true witness, who is the origin of all that God has created. I know what you have done; I know that you are neither cold nor hot. How I wish you were either one or the other! But because you are lukewarm, neither hot nor cold, I am going to spit you out of my mouth! You say, "I am rich and well off; I have all I need." But you do not know how miserable and pitiful you are! You are poor, naked, and blind. I advise you, then, to buy gold from me, pure gold, in order to be rich. Buy also white clothing to dress yourself and cover up your shameful nakedness. Buy also some ointment to put on your eyes, so that you can see. I rebuke and punish all whom I love. Be in earnest, then, and turn from your sins. Listen! I stand at the door and knock; if anyone hears my voice and opens the door, I will come into his house and eat with him, and he will eat with me.'

For years I envied some friends of ours whom we met shortly after we had got married. We were very hard up and they seemed by contrast to have a tremendous lifestyle. They had money and a beautiful house, and complimentary tickets to Ascot, London theatres and Lord's, first-class travel and a sumptuous car were just some of the perks that went with the husband's job.

Then one day he was made redundant. Just like that. Money was not an immediate problem; a generous pay-off saw to that.

But there was to be some grave fallout from the bomb that had hit them. Some of the effects were immediate, symbolized by the repossession of the company car. More bruises appeared over the next few weeks. Sleeplessness, fear for the future, moods swinging between anger and tears of inadequacy. And the inevitable questioning as to where he had gone wrong. All this was ghastly to see but the worst wound had yet to surface.

A few months afterwards my friend came to see me in a terrible state. 'Our marriage is over,' she sobbed. 'We've been together non-stop since he was made redundant and we've found we don't know each other at all any more and we certainly don't love each other.'

'But this is all such a shock for you both and you're both going through so much, I'm sure you'll be OK...' I fumbled on and on.

'You don't understand. We've not been close for years and we've both known it really but we've opted for a fun way of life and filled our lives so full that it hasn't worried us too much. He goes to work at six a.m. and doesn't get home till eight and on Sundays he plays golf so we only have to get on for one day a week at the most and usually we've got an invitation to dinner or tickets to a show so we haven't had to work at it at all. And it's all gone. The love? It must have crept out years ago. We never even saw it go—and now we need it it's not here.'

It was so sad and so final and it vaguely reminded me of something; the other day I was flicking through one of Adrian's books and I found a poem I asked him to write for me to perform years ago.

PHONE CALL

(Phone rings. Picks it up.)

Oh, Jesus? Don't come round tonight.
I'm busy at the hall
So chances of a chat with you are really rather small
Well, so many people need me and I can't deny them all

So... Looks as if I won't be in if you decide to call.
Tuesday? Would be better,
But I think the man next door
Is looking rather troubled... well I've helped him out
  before.
Friend in need, something you can never quite ignore
So, don't come round tomorrow night, you'll
  understand I'm sure.
Wednesday's our study night, Thursday I'm away
Friday? I've got tickets for the local Christian play
Saturday's the mission and that'll take all day
No, better that we leave it now till Sunday night, OK?

(Almost replaces receiver. Suddenly snatches it back to ear.)

Oh Jesus?... Do you love me?
Will you ever set me free?
I've built myself a prison.
I've thrown away the key.
I'm weeping in the darkness, Lord.
I'm longing now to see the plans you have for both
  of us.
Please come and visit me.

Let's face it. All our relationships need working on or they can become lukewarm. Especially our relationship with God. We can be so busy enjoying the worship, the speakers, the social life, the meetings (even the criticizing the leaders)—the whole caboodle that we call church—that we can end up, without realizing it, feeling 'I am rich and well off, I have all I need,' and forget completely about our personal relationship with our Father.

But if we are not spending time with him, expressing our needs, involving him in our stresses, crying all over him with joy and thanks, even grumbling at him sometimes, then this sort of blind self-sufficiency is inevitable. The greatest danger lies in the fact that the further away from him we get the less we feel we need him, the less we understand him and the less likely we are to want to sort out our relationship with him.

If that happens we may well find we have built ourselves a prison and thrown away the key.

There is always hope. Our friends' marriage didn't recover— but then one of the partners in it wasn't God! Just look at this amazing message communicated to us from the risen Lord Jesus through one of his closest friends left here on earth. He may be pretty fed up with the church in Laodicea but here he is offering to supply everything necessary to repair the broken relationship. As soon as we become concerned about the distance that has opened up between us and turn to him in earnest he is there for us. He will never force open the door but if we invite him to come in he will. He will sit down and eat with us and we will eat with him. Nothing will have changed at all.

PRAYER

Dear Father,

Please don't let us get so far away from you that our love grows cold. Hold us tight. Never let us go. We bring all our relationships to you now. We ask for your help and advice in those areas where things have gone wrong. Thank you for always being consistent in your love for us. Please come and visit us today. We'll try and have the door open for you. Amen.

BEWARE BLOODSUCKERS!

EXODUS 18:14–19, 24–27 (NIV)

When his father-in-law saw all that Moses was doing for the people, he said, 'What is this you are doing for the people? Why do you alone sit as judge while all these people stand round you from morning till evening?'

Moses answered him, 'Because the people come to me to seek God's will. Whenever they have a dispute, it is brought to me, and I decide between the parties and inform them of God's decrees and laws.'

Moses' father-in-law replied, 'What you are doing is not good. You and these people who come to you will only wear yourselves out. The work is too heavy for you; you cannot handle it alone. Listen now to me and I will give you some advice, and may God be with you...'

Moses listened to his father-in-law and did everything he said. He chose capable men from all Israel and made them leaders of the people, officials over thousands, hundreds, fifties and tens. They served as judges for the people at all times. The difficult cases they brought to Moses, but the simple ones they decided themselves. Then Moses sent his father-in-law on his way...

When I was writing about some of the things that Yuri told us during our memorable walk through the South African bush, I remembered another amazing story which at the time both Adrian and I felt was an all too apt parable of one of the ways in which we get exhausted and drained of energy. Our attention was drawn to a bush, which I remember as being about the height of a person, with lots of pretty silver leaves.

'This is called the Silver-Leafed Terminalia,' Yuri informed us. 'Can you see anything unusual about it?'

We peered at it hopefully, like children on a school trip peering at relics in a museum, and willed an intelligent answer to surface. All I could see was a bush whose beauty was marred by an ugly growth on one of its branches.

'It's got an ugly growth on one of its branches?' I tried.

'Exactly,' said Yuri, 'hence the Terminalia part of its name.'

He went on to tell us about the bush in more detail. Apparently this is a rather dimwitted example of African flora, which has difficulty in telling the difference between the egg laid in its bark by an insect and its own offspring. Thinking the egg to be a bud the proud but deluded parent plant pours all its energy into the 'bud's' growth. Sadly, what actually happens is that this food nurtures a growth that forms around the developing parasite. The plant, mistaking the increasingly ugly growth for a flower, tries even harder and concentrates even more goodies into that area, meanwhile denying itself vital nutrients and weakening sometimes to the point of death.

I think this parable is very much less obscure than some of those that Jesus used! Occasionally, I find myself utterly drained by the insatiable needs of some people and events. They seem to take an inordinate amount of my time and energy. Sometimes I am quite quite sure that that is exactly as it should be. I don't know where we would be today if at certain times in our lives we hadn't been given permission to drain the resources of our friends, or they ours, and I am equally sure that God expects us to go many very exhausting miles for him. I'm sure you will have experienced feeding and being fed in this way.

However, I do think that there is a danger that Christians can be trying so hard to get it right that they become deluded like the Silver-Leafed Terminalia. It has taken me many years to accept that occasionally we meet someone who is a parasite, greedily feeding off our energy until we are so weakened that we can no longer be of use. At this point people like this will often move on, looking for another confused, would-be 'parent' figure who will mistake their apparently innocent and desperate needs for something potentially beautiful, and therefore worth pouring out their lives for. (I find this really hard to write because I am so worried that people who have known me will interpret this as a comment on our relationship, but I can assure you that if you in any way think it could be you, it definitely can't, because parasites never question or doubt their motivation. They just feed!)

PRAYER

Father,

You know how muddled we get when we are trying to do your will. Please protect us from those who will use us up and spit us out, and give us discernment to know when you want us to lay down our daily lives and when you don't.

SECTION 2

THREE SPECIAL APPLES

The miracle of Lazarus being restored to life is so carefully stage-managed by Jesus, and so inextricably bound up with his eventual arrest, that it has always fascinated me. Partly because, like the wine at Cana, he has saved the best till last.

To raise a man from death a week after that death was perhaps the most spectacular of all Jesus' miracles. His relationship with the family; the proximity of Bethany to Jerusalem—with the inevitability of the miracle coming to the ears of the Sanhedrin—and the timing of the miracle just before Passover all add to the unique flavour of this public statement of the sovereignty of God.

COME ON IN!

L U K E   1 0 : 3 8   (N I V)

As Jesus and his disciples were on their way he came to a village where a woman named Martha opened her home to him.

I love the glimpses we are given of this little family. I'd give a lot to have been a fly on the wall while Mary and Martha were growing up. 'As different as chalk from cheese,' I can hear their mother say as she calms one stormy little girl and perhaps wishes the other could soften up a bit. Or praises the one for her diligence and despairs of the other's wild ways.

Now it's Martha's home, and Mary must have tried her patience something rotten! We don't meet Lazarus at this stage but he's in the picture somewhere, and having had two sons who for a while couldn't be in the same room without rubbing each other up the wrong way I sympathize with his inevitable role as peacemaker between his two sisters.

We know something else about this ordinary little family. We know that Jesus loved to pop in and eat with them when he was in Bethany. Perhaps he was able to feel off duty for a while, safely aware that what he said in their cosy kitchen would not be taken down and used in evidence against him. We know that despite his being seen by the crowds as rabbi and miracle-worker, and by the Pharisees as a major threat, Martha could speak to him as a friend and potential ally in her grumbling at Mary.

I wonder if they ever realized what their hospitality meant to this lonely Son of God while he was here, or what a privilege it was to have Jesus as that close a family friend.

Some years ago I was involved in facilitating a self-support group of women who were experiencing particularly acute problems in their home lives. I never ceased to be amazed at the courage and resilience they showed as they battled day by day with circumstances which would have finished me off.

As the weeks went by I was thrilled to see how well they were beginning to relate within the group and how openly they were sharing and advising each other. But one thing puzzled me. Despite their enthusiasm that they should support each other during the week as well as during our hour together, I discovered that they were not visiting each other in their homes at all. Distance was not the problem as they all lived on the same estate. Neither was time, as none of them were working.

At last I decided to tackle the subject. Apparently they had all without exception longed to do just that but felt embarrassed that their homes were not as nice as they would have liked them to be. One girl actually said that she had seen another member of the group crying as she pushed her two toddlers down the street and had longed to ask her in. But she was out of coffee and milk so had just watched her through the net curtains instead. After all this mutual confessing you can imagine there was a good deal of relieved laughter, and some really useful friendships began, some of which I know are still going on today.

Fear of being judged and feelings of inadequacy affect us all, don't they? Perhaps if we could feel confident enough to invite those who seem far above us into the very middle of our family ups and downs, and stop worrying about whether our home life is good enough, then we could share the privilege and give the same sense of belonging to another lonely child of God—which means, to Jesus himself.

PRAYER

Dear Father,

We so often feel we are not good enough to have much of a role in your plans. Forgive us for the times when we have let feelings like this hamper your loving work. Help us to stop peeping at the world through our net curtains and to throw open the doors of our lives and welcome you in. Amen.

GRACIOUS LIVING

LUKE 10:39–42 (NIV)

She had a sister called Mary, who sat at the Lord's feet listening to what he said. But Martha was distracted by all the preparations that had to be made. She came to him and asked, 'Lord, don't you care that my sister has left me to do the work by myself? Tell her to help me!'

'Martha, Martha,' the Lord answered, 'You are worried and upset about many things, but only one thing is needed. Mary has chosen what is better, and it will not be taken away from her.'

There was a particular day in my life that I think epitomizes the ludicrous pressure that women sometimes find themselves under.

It was Saturday morning and I was in the kitchen. On the work surfaces were rows of iceberg lettuce leaves each containing two quarters of tomato and three slices of cucumber. On our wooden kitchen table was a large dollop of marmalade, a half-drunk mug of tea and a plate containing the uneaten remains of a piece of toast. At the end of the table sat a disconsolate American eating lasagne and next to me stood a small girl wearing my black petticoat and a hopeful expression and holding a long scarf and several plastic necklaces.

Before you try and unravel the clues left at the scene of the crime, let me explain. The mini-salads were the result of a rash promise made at a recent church planning meeting. It was our fifth anniversary and we were celebrating it with a fun day and barbecue. I had suggested that instead of bowls of salad we could prepare these beforehand to make sure there was enough for everyone. Now everyone knows that you never suggest anything at a planning meeting unless you are prepared to do it yourself, so...!

The blob of marmalade was a protest gone wrong. I had said to one of my teenage sons that enough was enough and I wasn't his paid servant and from now on he would clear up his own breakfast mess. Fine as far as it went but after agreeing quite graciously to do it in a minute he had completely forgotten and gone out! I felt I should still make a stand so there the blob of marmalade had to stay.

The disconsolate American was a friend who had come to stay with us in order to work with my husband. The idyllic picture he had probably savoured of the two of them serenely being creative together was being shattered minute by minute and what was worse was that I had suddenly realized that I'd forgotten to give him any lunch and lumped him with the contents of the only container left in the freezer.

Lastly, the small girl was my daughter. That afternoon there was to be a fancy-dress parade based on characters from the Bible. For some obscure reason she had hit on the Queen of Sheba and felt strongly that my black shiny petticoat was exactly what she would have worn. By the time I had swirled the scarf round her head like a turban and she had covered herself with 'precious jewels' she looked somewhat vampish but by then I was too tired to care!

Why do we do it? Why don't we spend our time walking down dappled lanes or sipping Earl Grey on the terrace? Well maybe you do and if you do you'll have to give me the secret.

All I know is that life for many of us goes on at a ridiculous pace and we have far too little time to just 'be'. It wouldn't matter except that, without us really noticing, the quality of our lives begins to deteriorate and we lose confidence in our ability to do anything. What's more, having worked ourselves silly to come up to some unseen expectation, we end up letting someone or everyone down by being so exhausted that we forget something vital. Or else we end up feeling used and embittered, becoming surly and ungenerous with our time, forgiveness and understanding.

Either way there is little left of the inner joy that Jesus promised us.

Jesus recognized throughout his time with us the need to remove himself for short periods of time just to be with God. Admittedly all too often his time out was interrupted, but he returned to work refreshed from the time he had spent with his Father. But the self-imposed rule of a regular 'quiet time' has often become a pressure in itself for many people, failure to have it representing failure to come up to this same unseen expectation.

Time out for us to enjoy God in whatever setting relaxes us should perhaps be something we build in to every day. It could even mean a bit of dappled-lane walking!

In the meantime, if ever I write my autobiography (don't worry, I won't) it would have to be called *Fifty Salads and the Queen of Sheba*.

PRAYER

Father, please help us simply to stop.

Help us to learn how to relax with you, how to share our time with you. For those of us who have lost our joy we pray for refreshment. For those of us who have become hardened we pray for a softening of our hearts and an increased understanding of your love for us whether we do things for you or don't. Help us to choose wisely between the things that are important and the things that are of mini-salad importance so that we take control of our time. Draw us close to you. Thank you, Father. Amen.

'THE ONE YOU LOVE IS SICK'

JOHN 11:1–3 (NIV)

Now a man named Lazarus was sick. He was from Bethany, the village of Mary and her sister Martha. This Mary, whose brother Lazarus now lay sick, was the same one who poured perfume on the Lord and wiped his feet with her hair. So the sisters sent word to Jesus, 'Lord, the one you love is sick.'

I have been to so many different styles of prayer meeting in my Christian life and prayed in so many different ways for healing. One of my worst memories is this: a cold hall with a small uninviting circle of hard chairs in the middle and a tiny group of the most pessimistic people you could hope to meet. The list of the sick and dying took a long time to read because it was punctuated throughout by snippets of so-called news which in reality were snippets of gossip gleaned from bedsides with promises of secrecy.

That was bad enough. But it was followed by prayers spoken in a depressed whisper which cringingly asked God for a scrap of temporary comfort for the sick person as if the God they knew was too busy or mean to be bothered with anything else.

My other pet hate is the type of praying that consists of bellowing at God as though he is stone deaf, demanding, like petulant toddlers wanting sweets at the supermarket checkout counter, that the Holy Spirit come NOW. I'd never let my own children get what they wanted if they spoke to me like that so I don't really see why God should! It seems so rude, if you know what I mean. I've ended up in both those situations with a stiff bottom and a cross soul!

Not that it matters what I think. I learnt that a long time ago from a friend who had visited America on business. He told us of an experience he had had in an enormous church in California. He said he had been sitting there amazed and amused by the pretentiousness of the affair. There were artificial palm trees and massive bouffants of pink satin curtains and an enormous choir dressed to kill. He said he felt very righteous. What nonsense! How appalling! What must God think!

Suddenly he found out. Amid the noise of singing and shouted prayers he heard the sound of crying and turning round saw a young girl leave her wheelchair and dance for joy. Her parents were sobbing with incredulous joy. Looking round he saw other miracles taking place amid genuine rejoicing and he realized that all the razzmatazz didn't matter to God so long as hearts were truly turned to him.

This story has stayed with me ever since, and helped me to realize there is no value in judging the way different groups worship. The key isn't whether we have statues, crosses, cathedrals or church halls. Nor is it the virtues of the guitar versus the organ. The thing that God will see is the love in our hearts and that will be sweet music to his ears.

So I don't think it matters how we pray. But I think from now on I will take as my ideal style of praying for healing the message Mary and Martha sent to Jesus. What better prayer could there be than, 'Lord, the one you love is sick.' Their decision to send for Jesus was mutual and immediate. No begging, no extraneous details, just a confidence that he will want to be involved as a close friend, and that he will do something, because he loves them.

PRAYER

Dear Father,

You know us so well. You know how in a crisis we sometimes erect screens of panic and so for a while can't see you, and start talking to you in these strange ways. Help us to remember what Mary and Martha did. Increase our trust so that we can simply call you when we need you, knowing that whatever you decide to do you will have heard us.

PAINFUL SILENCE

J O H N   1 1 : 4 – 6   (N I V)

When he heard this, Jesus said, 'This sickness will not end in death. No, it is for God's glory so that God's Son may be glorified through it.' Jesus loved Martha and her sister and Lazarus. Yet when he heard that Lazarus was sick he stayed where he was two more days.

What must it have been like for Mary and Martha during the hours and then the days that followed the sending of their message? At first wondering whether the messenger has got there, talking confidently about what Jesus will do when he comes. I can imagine them running to the window every time they hear a sound of footsteps, straining their eyes down the dusty road trying to catch a glimpse of their beloved Jesus. Then the night coming and them lying in the dark, ears straining for the sound they are longing to hear. Then, gradually, hope giving way to increasing despair as they watch Lazarus weakening with all the terrible symptoms of a fatal illness.

What did they think then? Did they question the whole basis of their relationship with Jesus? Perhaps he didn't really love them as much as they'd thought. Perhaps he thought their request impertinent. Perhaps they shouldn't have sent for him.

Many of us know all too well how they must have felt because we've been there. We have waited, we have hammered at the doors of heaven, we have despaired and we have questioned whether the whole thing is some ghastly sick joke. Why isn't he here? Why doesn't he change things? Our confidence crumbles and the only salt we shed into the world is the salt in our tears.

Nothing in the world is more demoralizing than a long silence. Nothing seems to speak so eloquently of a broken relationship. Yet we know from experience too how misleading our feelings can be. I don't know how many children's stories I've read to children about bunnies or teddies who think everybody has forgotten their birthday—and then (after sad tears into outsize handkerchiefs) find that a surprise birthday tea complete with huge wobbly jellies and giant pink birthday cakes and a forest of beaming furry creatures awaits them. And I have known many lonely people who have misread busyness as avoidance and laziness or disorganization as a deliberate statement of indifference.

For some of us it isn't that simple. There is no equivalent of a table bulging with party food. The mystery of God's silence remains painfully unexplained this side of heaven. But there is something in this part of the story which just could help.

In the case of Mary and Martha it turns out that it was nothing to do with their relationship with Jesus but their small part of the huge complicated plan that would end in the crucifixion and the reconciliation of all humanity to their Father in heaven. What a mind-blowing thought. At the very point when we feel most deserted by God we may be acting out the starring role in our scene of the play whose final curtain will be the second coming.

Mind you, even knowing that, it can still hurt so much, can't it?

Dear Father,

There will be many of your children who even as they read this are screaming inside them, 'Why, why did you let this happen, God?' Few of us will ever understand why life has to be so confusingly hard for some people or why sometimes you choose to be silent. Please help them to see that it's not because you don't love them to pieces. Hold them close today, Father, and give those of us who stand helplessly watching and wondering the words of comfort and hope you would want them to hear from you.

LET US ALSO GO

JOHN 11:7–16 (NIV)

Then he said to his disciples, 'Let us go back to Judea.'

'But Rabbi,' they said, 'a short while ago the Jews tried to kill you, and yet you are going back there?'

Jesus answered, 'Are there not twelve hours of daylight? A man who walks by day will not stumble, for he sees by this world's light. It is when he walks by night that he stumbles, for he has no light.' After he had said this he went on to tell them, 'Our friend Lazarus has fallen asleep but I am going there to wake him up.'

His disciples replied, 'Lord, if he is asleep he will get better.' Jesus had been talking of his death, but his disciples thought he meant natural sleep. So then he told them plainly, 'Lazarus is dead and for your sake I am glad I was not there, so that you may believe. But let us go to him.'

Then Thomas (called Didymus) said to the rest of the disciples, 'Let us also go, that we may die with him.'

I have a horrible feeling that if I had been there I might have been one of the ones trying to persuade Jesus to stay away from Jerusalem. I can imagine their bewilderment at Jesus' apparent determination to travel to his potential doom just to wake up Lazarus from what they saw as a healing sleep. Or did they? Did they really misunderstand Jesus when he said that Lazarus had fallen asleep? It is so easy to convince ourselves that our motives are completely reasonable when we are frightened.

A child with a tummy ache before a worrying day at school believes in that tummy ache totally. The proof of the illness can only be revealed when the time for the school starting bell is past and the child is safely and cosily at home. Since children are unversed in subterfuge, wild bed trampolining is the favourite sign of the famous vanishing tummy ache trick! The headache we wake with before facing a particularly difficult day at work is definitely going to turn into a migraine—while we are sure a paracetamol will sort it out if we are looking forward to the day ahead. I don't think that's villainy. But this sort of self-delusion can have more serious consequences.

I have far too often convinced myself that I have no time to contact an acquaintance when the truth is that I find phoning anyone really difficult. Fewer ministers seem to feel God's leading to Brixton than they do to Bath. Many more people seem to hear God calling them to go on a prayer march round a disturbed council estate than calling them to work in it. And from personal experience I can tell you that many people working with disturbed teenagers find that the sort of language they hear so defiles their temple of the Holy Spirit that they feel quite sure they should not continue to work in such an environment. We are so very fallible, aren't we?

The disciples were facing far more than a bad day at school or a swearing teenager. Thank heavens for Thomas. Incidentally, don't you love the fact that it was this particular disciple, famous only for his doubting, who faced his fears openly and offered Jesus the support he needed?

PRAYER

Dear Father,

Please let the Holy Spirit come and sit beside us throughout today, and to help us to look honestly at our motivation in all the decisions we are making. Please don't let us prevent anyone from doing the

job you have for them because of our own fears, selfishness or jealousy.

Thank you for Thomas. Through what we know about him, help us to see how easily we judge, basing our opinions on just one small part of someone's behaviour in the past.

Today could get a bit uncomfortable, Lord. But please don't let us get away with not being ruthless with ourselves in these areas.

LET PEOPLE BE REAL

J O H N   1 1 : 1 7 - 2 0

On his arrival, Jesus found that Lazarus had already been in the tomb for four days. Bethany was less than two miles from Jerusalem, and many Jews had come to Mary and Martha to comfort them in the loss of their brother. When Martha heard that Jesus was coming, she went out to meet him but Mary stayed at home.

In the wonderful children's story *The Velveteen Rabbit*, the toys Skin Horse and Rabbit have an in-depth discussion about what it means to be Real. In answer to Rabbit's question about whether it hurts to become Real, Skin Horse replies 'Sometimes,' and goes on to explain that ' "It doesn't happen all at once... It takes a long time. That's why it doesn't often happen to people who break easily or have sharp edges, or who have to be carefully kept. Generally by the time you are Real, most of your hair has been loved off and your eyes drop out and you get loose in the joints and very shabby. But these things don't matter at all because once you are Real you can't be ugly except to people who don't understand..." Rabbit sighed. He longed to become Real... he wished he could become it without these uncomfortable things happening to him.'

I have several friends who are involved with Cruse, the counselling service offered to those who have been bereaved. One of the things they try to emphasize is that no two people grieve the same but the key is to be true to oneself. Mary and Martha were equally devastated by their brother's death, but here is

Martha rushing down the road to give Jesus a piece of her mind full of blinding indignation and Mary sobbing at home, needing to be alone in her grief.

I mentioned this to a friend of mine whose husband died recently and she immediately identified with Mary. Only now, six months later, is she able to be with people without risking breaking down. I know someone else who the day after her beloved husband died joined a charity shop because she needed to be busy and be with as many people as possible. Quite clearly there is no *right* way and Jesus' reaction to both of his dear friends shows that he loved them and empathized with them equally.

PRAYER

Dear Father,

It is so easy for us to think we *know* what someone else should do or feel because of our own reaction to a situation. Help us to clear our thoughts of all our assumptions and spend time today listening to you so that if there is some tiny way in which we can be of real use to you we won't miss it because we are so busy thinking of ways to impress on someone what we think they should do and how we think they should be. Amen.

LET IT ALL OUT

JOHN 11:20−27 (NIV)

When Martha heard that Jesus was coming, she went out
to meet him, but Mary stayed at home.

'Lord,' Martha said to Jesus, 'if you had been here, my
brother would not have died. But I know that even now
God will give you whatever you ask.'

Jesus said to her, 'Your brother will rise again.'

Martha answered, 'I know he will rise again in the
resurrection at the last day.'

Jesus said to her, 'I am the resurrection and the life. He
who believes in me will live, even though he dies; and
whoever lives and believes in me will never die. Do you
believe this?'

'Yes, Lord,' she told him, 'I believe that you are the
Christ, the Son of God, who was to come into the world.'

I love this woman! Never again let her be denigrated as boring. I love thinking of her ripping off her pinny, banging the door behind her and lifting her skirts to run down the road to meet Jesus and have it out with him.

In one breath she tears her friend off a strip for not getting there in time to save her brother and in the next reveals amazing faith in her master. The fact that Lazarus has been dead for four days might justifiably have dinted her confidence just a bit but she says, 'I know that even now God will give you whatever you ask' and then shows both her understanding of the scriptures and prophetic discernment that Jesus is the Christ, the Son of God.

I can't help wishing that we were able like Martha to run down the road and actually meet Jesus face to face when crises overwhelm us. Whatever Martha might have felt before she met him obviously evaporated in the solidity of his presence. Suddenly everything was going to be all right because he was there at last.

I know lots of people who have a few things planned to say to God when they meet him, myself included! Even as I'm writing this I'm battling through a good deal of anger and confusion about the premature death of a dear friend—and all over Britain people are trying to come to terms with the fact that a gunman has just mowed down a classroom of infants in a primary school in Scotland.

I don't think there's much point in trying to come up with a neat spiritual solution to such a ghastly, needless tragedy. But I think we *can* hurl our bewilderment at God. Where were you? How could you let this happen? Don't you care? Can't you see that this is the sort of thing that turns potential followers away and causes your little ones to stumble?

My only comfort in times like this is the knowledge that whenever someone actually met Jesus in the middle of their despair something about him restored their hope—and somehow inspired complete trust that he was in it with them.

PRAYER

Dear Father,

We need to talk to you today. We need to tell you in no uncertain terms how we feel about something that has happened in our lives or in the lives of friends of ours. Thank you that you listened so lovingly to Martha's honest and hurting outburst. Please listen to us today as we allow our deep feelings of bewilderment to be voiced, possibly after a long time of keeping them bottled up inside us. Help us to allow ourselves to be held by you at last.

JESUS WEPT

JOHN 11:28-29, 32-35

And after she had said this, she went back and called her sister Mary aside. 'The teacher is here,' she said, 'and is asking for you. When Mary heard this, she got up quickly and went to him... When Mary reached the place where Jesus was and saw him, she fell at his feet and said, 'Lord, if you had been here, my brother would not have died.'

When Jesus saw her weeping and the Jews who had come along with her also weeping, he was deeply moved in spirit and troubled. 'Where have you laid him?' he asked.

'Come and see, Lord,' they replied.

Jesus wept.

Why? Why did he weep? Surely he knew that everything was going to be all right for his favourite family?

Was it because he felt guilty that he could have prevented their pain by coming earlier but because he needed Lazarus' healing to be a major miracle they had had to suffer? Or because he knew that what he was about to do was the beginning of his own long journey towards death? Or because he knew, as God's son, that whatever he said they could not understand? Or quite simply because he couldn't bear to see his dear friends in such agony? Whatever the reason, I'm so very glad he did weep.

Sometimes, especially since being a parent, I've found myself in a situation where I've known that someone's grief will only be temporary. I've plastered grazed knees and tried unsuccessfully to mend favourite toys. I've cuddled to sleep a toddler devastated by the loss of a one-eared soft rabbit. I've attended funerals of budgies and hamsters. I've watched helplessly the agony caused by the betrayal of a best friend who chooses to sit next to someone else on the coach. I've touched fingers in sympathy at an unsuccessful audition. I've listened to the thudding grief of a small mud-plastered footballer who has just scored an own goal. And I've been there myself.

I've learnt slowly that passing on knowledge that their grief will be temporary, in the form of 'Never mind. You'll get over it,' is useless and can be damaging. Yes, the pain will lessen in time. It may even go completely. But right now they are hurting and they can't understand and nothing will ever be the same again.

If you are in that situation now, needing arms round you and needing to know that someone who loves you is sitting in the dark with you, remember that Jesus wept. He knew he was going to heal Lazarus. But still he wept. He will never minimize your pain. Just as he was asking for Mary, who had shut herself away from everyone in her grief, so he is asking for you. Let him weep with you.

PRAYER

Dear Father,

You know us so well. You know the pain that is bleeding its way through our heads and hearts. You know the panic and loneliness that comes from feeling that there is no one who can or who wants to understand. Help us to uncurl from our dark corner and turn to you. Help us to tell you all the little things that she or he said, or didn't say. Help us to look at you, so we can see your tears.

'TAKE AWAY THE STONE!'

JOHN 11:38-42 (NIV)

Jesus, once more deeply moved, came to the tomb. It was a cave with a stone laid across the entrance. 'Take away the stone,' he said.

'But, Lord,' said Martha, the sister of the dead man, 'by this time there is a bad odour, for he has been there four days.'

Then Jesus said, 'Did I not tell you that if you believed you would see the glory of God?'

So they took away the stone. Then Jesus looked up and said, 'Father I thank you that you have heard me. I knew that you always hear me but I said this for the benefit of the people standing here that they may believe that you sent me.'

Some of us have problems that stink. I know that this is an extremely distasteful image, but I have met people who have unresolved horrors which have been festering for years, locked inside tombs by boulders which are immovable. Or which seem immovable.

Some people are all too aware that the poison is beginning to seep through the cracks and threaten their security—even their sanity. Others refuse to admit there is anything behind the boulder and desperately camouflage the entrance, terrified of how they'd cope if what was in there was ever discovered. Some have been convinced by others that their problem is not really deep-seated at all and that it could easily be removed if it wasn't for their stubbornness.

If ever there was an illustration that no problem is too big for God this has to be it. There is a sense that this is for Jesus a test case, an amazing visual reminder for the disciples in particular but also for all those there present that God is a God of power as well as of love. That is something they will need to hang on to over the next few weeks as they wrestle with the powerlessness of their Lord in the hands of the Pharisees.

Even before arriving at Bethany Jesus had stated that what was to happen was to glorify God. And he seems to have deliberately stayed away to create a situation which was apparently totally insoluble.

The reaction of the disciples is quite understandable. We react in the same way today. We still seem to have a social code which determines what is acceptable to God and what he can and can't do. This reflects our feelings of inadequacy and our inability to cope. Where two or three gather together in his name they do rather frequently find that (surprise surprise) they all know that God agrees entirely with their decision to ditch, postpone or reflect the problem onto the bearer of the problem.

I base this on years of involvement with residential social work. This is the pattern. A child arrives who has displayed such appalling problem behaviour in his or her last placement that a meeting has been held where it has been decided that, in the best interests of the child (and nothing whatsoever to do with the fact that the child has used up all the resources of the social workers and made them feel stupid) she or he should move on to another establishment.

On arrival the child is assured that they will be allowed to stay long-term and that this is the ideal place for them. Three months later another meeting is held. It is agreed, with a deep sense of serious consideration for the child's well-being, that she or he should be moved to another establishment—nothing whatsoever to do with the fact that the child has used up all the resources of the social workers and made them feel stupid!!

This isn't meant to be funny. Being considered too difficult to cope with may give the child a short burst of feelings of power and it will certainly give him or her a reputation which has to be upheld. However, it will also increase the terror that what they have within them is so awful that no one can help.

The result is twofold: a terrifying escalation of the behaviour which caused the expulsion and increasing isolation from those in authority who have lost the chance they had earlier on to roll away the boulder and deal with the poison within.

I have a young friend who has been made to feel like some sort of freak because the problem she has (not in any way of her own making) has proved too big for the leaders of her church. 'They said they couldn't cope with me,' she sobbed one night. 'Am I so awful, so dirty, that not even God wants to know?'

Of course we don't always know what to do. I sometimes think I never do! Some problems are so deep-seated that they need someone who is skilled in that particular area to work with the person—and if we start trying to do something we might only make things worse. But this is quite a different thing from suggesting that God either can't deal with it, doesn't want to get his hands dirty, or doesn't love the person enough to want to.

PRAYER

Dear Father,

Here we are again, out of our depth! Give us the courage today to begin to roll away the boulder that we have placed over the entrance to our deep-seated unresolved problems and allow you to see into the darkness within. Increase our trust in you that you will not be shocked or disgusted by anything that you will find. Help us to believe in your love and wisdom so that slowly, and with you

next to us, we can begin to seek appropriate help and eventually allow our lives to be washed clean in your waters of healing.

PLEASE TAKE CHARGE

JOHN 11:43–45 (NIV)

When he had said this, Jesus called in a loud voice, 'Lazarus, come out!' The dead man came out, his hands and feet wrapped with strips of linen, and a cloth around his face.
   Jesus said to them, 'Take off the grave clothes and let him go.'

It's not easy being an onlooker. It's not comfortable feeling helpless. But what can we do to avoid the feelings of inadequacy that lead us into the sort of temptation mentioned yesterday? I've always struggled with this. Adrian, my husband, says that when he first met me I was rushing around my friends with a metaphorical mop and bucket trying to clear up problems I had no hope of solving.

Several years ago a dear friend went through the horror of her husband leaving her for another woman. Having been brought up to believe that a Christian marriage was bound somehow to work out she was completely shattered. Why had it happened? How could God have let it happen? Where had she gone wrong? Why had no one told her? What sort of person was she, was he?

I felt so very helpless. I so much wanted to sort it out for her, to take away the agony which she was carrying and to restore the confidence which had been shattered. Helplessly I watched her, in order to cope with her daily life and to care for her child, pushing the pain further and further inside, placing a boulder over the entrance. For once my desperation led me to face my limitations honestly.

'I want to say that I'll be there for you whenever you need me,' I said, 'but I know that I won't. I know I'll let you down. I know there'll be times in the middle of the night when you'll be totally alone and desperate and I won't even be aware of it. I want to take away your pain but I know I'll say the wrong thing, do the wrong thing. I'll forget to pray. But I do love you and I will do my best.'

It was the best thing I could have done. Both of us felt freed from the pressure of coping better than we were capable of. And I learnt one of the most valuable lessons of my life. Yes, there are lots of situations too big for us to sort out. We can't take away the pain. We don't perform miracles. But there are lots of things we can do in helping to roll away the stone. Some of them are clear from this passage.

We can ask God to help. We can listen, watch and pray so that when the time comes we can join in appropriately with what he wants us to do. We can seek expert help and become involved with the frightening business of looking for the first time at the source of the smell. If and when healing does occur we can help, slowly and gently, to take off the grave clothes, the grubby remnants of fear and panic that still cling. Then we can trust the person and support them and encourage their independence from us. And we can be a friend, however costly that turns out to be.

PRAYER

Dear Father,

Today let me stand back and allow you to take control of all aspects of the things that trouble me. Help me to accept my role in it all, passing whichever surgical instrument you need passing to you. Please don't let me blunder in and mess up what you are doing and please prevent me from offering more than I can manage either in the area of expertise or time. Yes, Father, take charge of all that I do today.

USE GOD'S GIFT

JOHN 12:1 – 4

Six days before the Passover, Jesus went to Bethany, the home of Lazarus, the man he had raised from death. They prepared a dinner for him there, which Martha helped to serve; Lazarus was one of those who were sitting at the table with Jesus. Then Mary took half a litre of a very expensive perfume made of pure nard, poured it on Jesus' feet, and wiped them with her hair. The sweet smell of the perfume filled the whole house.

What a heady mixture of joy and pain there must have been that night in Bethany. The two sisters have prepared a banquet to say thank you to their dear friend, and seated with him and the disciples is the brother he has so wonderfully restored to them. So much to celebrate.

Yet how hollow their rejoicing must have seemed, aware as they were of the swelling atmosphere of hatred towards Jesus. What must have seemed so awful was that it was coming from some of the Jews who had witnessed the miracle of Lazarus being brought back to life. How bewildering that something so obviously motivated by love might have proved the final straw for those jealous of his increasing popularity. Rumour had it that even Lazarus' life was at stake.

What was to become of them all? Would this be the last night they would spend eating, talking and laughing together round the dinner table, the last time Martha would fuss around and wait on them, the last time that a special silence would fall as

Jesus began one of those wonderful stories...?

Suddenly Martha's contrivance at normality proves too much for Mary and she abandons all sense of propriety, impulsively pouring her most precious ointment over the feet of her Lord and wiping his feet with her hair. Oh, Mary, what else matters but that he knows you understand and what better way for you to show him than to sacrifice your reputation and your most prized possession in one glorious moment of worship? How he must have loved you at that moment—not for what you did but just for being so 'you'. The room was filled with fragrance, we are told.

I don't know about you, but I've sometimes been in situations where I've known that at a precise moment I have in my possession a jar of priceless balm. I have intuitively within me the words, the understanding, or the gesture that could fill the room with the fragrance of healing or compassion or forgiveness. But I have chosen to bring my jar home unbroken. Maybe I was afraid to make a fool of myself or I was unsure of how my gesture would be received. Maybe I didn't care quite enough or I was angry or indifferent or sulky. Whatever the motivation I missed my chance to perform a vital task for God, a task divinely suited to my personality.

If I'm honest I don't think the Church celebrates sufficiently gifts from the more impulsive personalities in their midst. They can be made to feel clumsy and inappropriate in many situations where the Marthas of this world fit easily. And their sins do often tend to be rather obvious. They don't so much fall as plummet! But God has given them some of his loveliest presents, knowing they will share them generously. Being a bit of a Mary myself, crashing through life making untold mistakes, I take great joy in realizing that on this poignant night she got it absolutely right.

PRAYER

Dear Father,

Help us to look today at the contents of our balm jar. What do we have in our possession that we could spill generously for you? Is there a situation where we have deliberately withheld even a precious ounce of word or gesture that should have been giving comfort and support? We are so very sorry, Father. Please give us another chance to use the unique gift that you have given each one of us in the way you would like.

THE MOMENT IS ALL

JOHN 12:4−11 (NIV)

But one of his disciples, Judas Iscariot, who was later to betray him, objected, 'Why wasn't this perfume sold and the money given to the poor? It was worth a year's wages.' He did not say this because he cared about the poor but because he was a thief; as keeper of the money bag, he used to help himself to what was put into it.

'Leave her alone,' Jesus replied. 'It was meant that she should save this perfume for the day of my burial. You will always have the poor among you, but you will not always have me.'

Meanwhile a large crowd of Jews found out that Jesus was there and came, not only because of him but also to see Lazarus, whom he had raised from the dead. So the chief priests made plans to kill Lazarus as well, for on account of him many of the Jews were going over to Jesus and putting their faith in him.

This is interesting, isn't it? Taken out of context it could give the health–and–wealth fanatics a bit of a boost—Jesus himself saying, 'You will always have the poor among you...' Pretty extraordinary. Surely Judas had a point. And yet, and yet. This is the same Jesus that throughout his three years of ministry sought out the weak, the poor, the suffering, the outcasts of society. The beatitudes make it quite clear what he thought about the poor and vulnerable.

What we are seeing here is the glorious truth that every

situation we find ourselves in is unique however many times we find ourselves in it. And just occasionally we are going to be asked to step out of our normal routine and do something quite wonderfully bizarre. Just as Paul only once felt it was right to change course completely and go to Macedonia when it made logical sense to carry on to Bithynia. So nine times out of ten it is right to obey the general rules of charity and common sense laid down over and over again by Jesus. This one occasion was different.

In 1995 we visited Soweto, attending one of several daily worship meetings in a mission tent led by Nick Misupi. Words cannot describe the surging joy, the heartfelt emotion and the glorious pounding singing that shook the tent, which literally bulged at the seams. When Adrian had the opportunity to tell the congregation what a privilege it was for us to worship with our brothers and sisters in Soweto the roar of 'Amen' practically flattened the tent!

Afterwards, on receiving confirmation that it was all right to do so, we used up yards of film on the church children—and their beaming, open smiles remind us of this enchanting time from a frame on our living-room mantelpiece.

But one photo means more to me than any of these. It is a photo of a pile of mattresses, chairs, radios, bikes and innumerable other objects piled to the ceiling in a little store room behind the tent. When Nick showed us this his huge Zulu face shone with joy. Apparently after each meeting the new converts (and there are up to fifty a day) receive counselling. They are taught that the cost of following Jesus is huge and that as a symbol of their new life they must return all the goods they have stolen from the white man and hand in their guns.

The guns are handed over to the police and the goods are collected in this little room and once a week they are burned. A symbol of dying to sin and beginning a new life. All of our family were profoundly moved by this and Adrian wrote about it in a regular letter he does for the Bible Society. He received one very angry reply from a lady who felt very upset about his condoning what seemed to her a waste of valuable resources. For her it was obvious that the goods should be distributed to the poor and needy.

For a moment, when I read the letter, I was filled with confusion. What was Nick thinking of? Immediately afterwards I knew. The whole of his ministry and that of his associate pastors was committed, Jesus-like, to relieving the hurts of the poor. But to distribute these goods would have been quite wrong. They were stolen. They represented an old way of life. They stood for sin renounced. However useful a resource they might have been, on this one occasion it was right to waste them.

So, back to Mary and her precious nard. On this unique occasion rules needed to be broken and the forthcoming sacrifice acknowledged extravagantly. Just for a moment the poor must wait. The moment was all.

And so to us. To perpetually generous nard-slingers there will be times when the godly exception to our rule is to show restraint. To the frugal steward there will be occasions when the right thing to do is a touch of nard-slinging. There will be God-given opportunities for each of us to enhance the occasions we find ourselves in. To have an open ear to the Holy Spirit is the way to discover what they are. But I think we may be surprised by what he will be asking us to do!

PRAYER

Open our ears, Lord.

Help us to listen today to what the Holy Spirit is asking us to do for you, however surprising we may feel it to be. Amen.

COURAGE TO BE WEAK

JOHN 12:42−43 (NIV)

Yet at the same time many even among the leaders believed in him. But because of the Pharisees they would not confess their faith for fear they would be put out of the synagogue; for they loved the praise of men more than praise from God.

Oh dear, I feel this really hits at the heart of the reason for most of us not confessing our faith more publicly. We all have synagogues which for one reason or another we don't want to be cast out of and some of us even have our own pet Pharisee who would take great pleasure in instigating our removal. Obviously for Jewish leaders at the time of Jesus, being put out of the synagogue would have serious consequences. At least it would hardly be viewed as a good career move. For most of us the worst it means is that from then on we might be identified with the ridiculous stereotypes that television sitcoms excel at. So why does it matter to us so much?

A little while ago I had an interesting opportunity to discover just how pathetic I am. I was taking part in a course designed to retrain me as a primary teacher. It was the first time for some years that I found myself among a large group of people who were not necessarily connected with Christianity and I was loving every minute of it. The only slight anxiety I had was that it was obvious from what several of them had said that the overall opinion of the Church was very low.

I felt a bit guilty but I was so enjoying making new friends and being back in what felt like mainstream living that I convinced myself that just for once I didn't need to defend the Church, so long as no one attacked what I actually believed. For some time I had been thought of as simply an appendage to my husband's Christian writing and speaking, and it was just so nice being accepted purely for myself. I told you it was pretty pathetic!

Anyway, one morning the subject of our lecture was teaching RE. I was fascinated to hear what would be expected of us as primary teachers but was totally unprepared for the lecturer's first remarks. 'This is a controversial subject and before I talk in detail about what the national curriculum syllabus consists of I would like to hear your views on the subject. I am going to go round the room and give each of you a chance to air your views.'

Here it was at last. My opportunity to tell everyone about my faith. So why did I feel sick? Why was my heart pounding against my ribs and my tongue dry? I was hardly going to be thrown to the lions. These people were my friends. Anyway, I was proud of what I believed. It was my chance to proclaim the gospel. What on earth was the matter with me?

By the time it was my turn to speak I was so nervous I could only whisper. Of course I was very relieved after I had managed to state how important my relationship with Jesus was—and afterwards there was nothing terribly different about the way people treated me. But I knew that there was a gap. Apart from apologizing for anything they thought might offend me there was a sort of unspoken sympathy for me.

I had become in their eyes one of those strange, sad people who need the prop of religion or who had been brainwashed into believing something they in their wisdom knew to be nonsense. I have a friend who has been involved for many years in the area of abuse survival. She tells me that the group will tolerate anyone coming to speak to them except Christians, for these very reasons.

I appreciate that my experience was very slight by contrast with the horrendous aggression many Christians have to face in the workplace and at home. But I remember clearly enough the ridicule I sometimes had to cope with years ago during my time as a child care worker.

Being associated with weakness is always difficult and there is no doubt that for the vast majority being a Christian today carries little kudos. It is seen as either stuffy and irrelevant or ridiculous and ineffective. Then there is the fact that we are trying to voluntarily lay down the weapons of aggressive response, and our new ammunition of absorbing attack and trying to forgive seem puny in the world's fluorescent light.

But maybe it's more fundamental than that. We all desperately need to be liked and accepted and the fact is that you can actually *hear* the praise of men while you have to *trust* in the praise of God!

PRAYER

Dear Father,

Help us to remember that we have something to be really proud of, something worth being put out of synagogues for. Give us courage to laugh in the face of demeaning insults and patronizing sympathy. Forgive us for the times when we have left your side in order to be accepted by a group of those who don't know you. Amen.

SECTION 3

'YES' TO ADVENTURE

There's a bit of a taboo developing over the very mention of Mary in some sections of the Protestant Church. It feels like another example of throwing the baby out with the bath-water. In our determination to show how unimpressed we are with her position as 'most prayed-to saint' in the Catholic Church we seem unable to look at her at all. When we do mention her in a sort of obligatory way before Christmas it is often her quality of meekness that is emphasized, and the fact that she is usually represented in primary-school nativity plays by the smallest and sweetest little girl available does nothing to dispel this myth.

I personally think that, as well as being a very special apple of her heavenly Father's eye, she is one of the toughest and most courageous disciples that her son and Saviour ever had. So let's give her a chance, out of the context of Christmas, to teach us what being a child of God and a disciple of Jesus is about.

'YES' TO ADVENTURE

LUKE 1:26–38

In the sixth month of Elizabeth's pregnancy God sent the angel Gabriel to a town in Galilee named Nazareth. He had a message for a girl promised in marriage to a man named Joseph, who was a descendant of King David. The girl's name was Mary. The angel came to her and said, 'Peace be with you! The Lord is with you and has greatly blessed you!'

Mary was deeply troubled by the angel's message, and she wondered what his words meant. The angel said to her, 'Don't be afraid, Mary; God has been gracious to you. You will become pregnant and give birth to a son, and you will name him Jesus. He will be great and will be called the Son of the Most High God. The Lord God will make him a king, as his ancestor David was, and he will be the king of the descendants of Jacob for ever; his kingdom will never end!'

Mary said to the angel, 'I am a virgin. How, then, can this be?'

The angel answered, 'The Holy Spirit will come on you, and God's power will rest upon you. For this reason the holy child will be called the Son of God. Remember your relative Elizabeth. It is said that she cannot have children, but she herself is now six months pregnant, even though she is very old. For there is nothing that God cannot do.'

'I am the Lord's servant,' said Mary; 'may it happen to me as you have said.' And the angel left her.

This girl should never again be depicted as docile. She was clearly young and she was a virgin but docility and virginity do not automatically go together. Neither do docility and youth. (I don't think they ever did.)

In agreeing to this extraordinary request she showed a courage as great as any displayed throughout the Bible. Gabriel doesn't tell her he's going to speak to Joseph on her behalf. He doesn't promise anything actually. She is being asked to risk her marriage, her reputation, possibly even her life! Yet her immediate response is a resounding 'yes'. No fleeces like Gideon. No excuses like Moses. Just yes.

To accept the challenge that God gives us without knowing what lies in store for us seems so often to be God's way. Abraham had to set out on his long journey without knowing where he was going. Noah had to build a boat despite the ridicule of his neighbours.

Some years ago Adrian and I had the joy of meeting David Watson several times before his death. On the first occasion that we met he had just been diagnosed as having cancer. He described his slow but determined progress towards accepting the possibility that he might die while wanting desperately to be healed. He wanted to be able to say yes to whatever God had in store for him and by the time we met him again he had done so.

'The best is yet to come' was the phrase that we will never forget. He had moved to a point where he was looking forward to death but was prepared to stay if that was God's will. He had chosen to say, like Mary, 'I am the Lord's servant, may it happen to me as you have said.'

As a woman something I find very reassuring about the whole dialogue between Mary and Gabriel is the fact that God has chosen to deal directly with her. Joseph is not asked his opinion first. Her father does not even get a mention. I find that in some sections of the Church today many married women have been led to feel that, because of the husband's role as 'head of the woman', their relationship with their heavenly Father is in some way secondary to that of their husband, and that God is hardly likely to speak to them first.

There are terrible dangers in this. Unless our relationship is directly with God everything can easily get out of sorts. We can place too much expectation on our husband's bringing us news from God. We can end up bitter and resentful, and above all we can lose sight of our Father's love for us and of how special we are in his sight.

Mary herself was spoken to, and it is clear from her reply that she already had a mature love for her Lord and a desire to be obedient to him whatever the cost. Obviously one of the reasons she was selected was her forthcoming marriage to a descendant of David, but there would have been hundreds of such women to choose from over the years. No, quite clearly Mary was chosen for herself, and equally clearly she has the option to accept the job or not. The fact that Gabriel only departs after she has spoken shows that her reply was important. It was not going to happen to her unless she agreed.

A few years ago I was in charge of a small youth group that met in my house after church. As a discussion starter one evening I had prepared a questionnaire in which they had to give marks out of ten for some things they hoped to have in the future. Included in the list were money, a career, a family and adventure. I was stunned to find one girl had given adventure no marks at all. Nought for adventure!

Mary, at much the same age, has given it ten.

Dear Father,

We so want to be able to say 'yes' to whatever you have planned for us. Please help us to overcome those things that prevent us. For some of us it is fear of the unknown; for some it is lack of confidence that you could possibly have a job for us to do; for some it is that we haven't yet learnt how to listen to you. Help us today to move a little closer to the time when we too can give ten marks to adventure.

HELP US REJOICE

LUKE 1:39−56

Soon afterwards Mary got ready and hurried off to a town in the hill-country of Judaea. She went into Zechariah's house and greeted Elizabeth. When Elizabeth heard Mary's greeting, the baby moved within her. Elizabeth was filled with the Holy Spirit and said in a loud voice, 'You are the most blessed of all women, and blessed is the child you will bear! Why should this great thing happen to me, that my Lord's mother comes to visit me? For as soon as I heard your greeting, the baby within me jumped with gladness. How happy you are to believe that the Lord's message to you will come true!'

Mary said,
'My heart praises the Lord;
my soul is glad because of God my Saviour,
for he has remembered me, his lowly servant!
From now on all people will call me happy,
because of the great things the Mighty God has done for
* me.*
His name is holy;
from one generation to another
he shows mercy to those who honour him.
He has stretched out his mighty arm
and scattered the proud with all their plans
He has brought down mighty kings
from their thrones,
and lifted up the lowly.
He has filled the hungry with good things,

and sent the rich away with empty hands.
He has kept the promise he made to our ancestors,
and has come to the help of his servant Israel.
He has remembered to show mercy to Abraham
and to all his descendants for ever!'
   Mary stayed about three months with Elizabeth and
then went back home.

It cannot be insignificant that Gabriel mentioned Elizabeth's pregnancy to her young cousin and then immediately afterwards we hear that Mary has hurried off to find Elizabeth and spend time with her. In times of crisis we all need someone special who will understand what we are going through. Sometimes it is a member of our family but more often it is someone who is in or has been in the same situation as ourselves. Most self-support groups operate on that basis.

Mary has been told that Elizabeth is in much the same boat as herself, a miracle baby growing inside both of them, and it must have seemed a literal Godsend to be able to spend time with someone so able to empathize.

What a meeting it was. These two ordinary women bursting with babies and the Holy Spirit. What confidence must have flooded into the young visitor at Elizabeth's words. Here was recognition that she had been right to trust the angel's message. Here was the confirmation she needed that it was all true, that she really was to be the mother of her Lord.

This is a very special part of the whole story to me. I love the idea of the unborn baby John thumping about in his mother's womb with excitement. What a Spirit-filled character he was, even then. I love to think of Elizabeth, made young again by the pregnancy that (in her own words) had taken away her disgrace, ministering to a girl who was possibly going to have to face an even greater disgrace on her return.

I love Mary's girlish excitement at what is happening to her. Not a word about the problems. Just a glorious outpouring of joy and praise. But more than all this I love the fact that God gave them this precious time together. Both women are going to lose their sons at an early age. Both will be deprived of the joy of shedding tears at their sons' weddings. Neither are going to be grandmothers. The sacrifice they are both going to be called on to make is huge. But for now, nestled in the hills of Judea, they can be happy and safe.

PRAYER

Dear Father,

We know that in order for your will to be accomplished here on earth you need willing servants. We thank you for Mary and Elizabeth who dedicated their lives and the lives of their children to you so completely. Help us to be prepared to do the same if you want us to. Help us to rejoice in the task you have given us to do whatever the cost—and thank you for the friends you have provided for us in our times of crisis. Amen.

NOT JUNK MAIL... BUT REALITY

LUKE 2:1, 3−12, 15−16

At that time the Emperor Augustus ordered a census to be taken throughout the Roman Empire... Every one then went to register himself each to his own town. Joseph went from the town of Nazareth in Galilee to the town of Bethlehem in Judaea, the birthplace of King David. Joseph went there because he was a descendant of David. He went to register with Mary, who was promised in marriage to him. She was pregnant and while they were in Bethlehem, the time came for her to have her baby. She gave birth to her first son, wrapped him in strips of cloth and laid him in a manger—there was no room for them to stay in the inn.

There were some shepherds in that part of the country who were spending the night in the fields taking care of their flocks. An angel of the Lord appeared to them and the glory of the Lord shone over them. They were terribly afraid, but the angel said to them... 'This very day in David's town your Saviour was born—Christ the Lord. And this is what will prove it to you: you will find a baby wrapped in strips of cloth and lying in a manger.'... When the angels went away from them back to heaven, the shepherds said one to another, 'Let's go to Bethlehem and see this thing that has happened, which the Lord has told us.'

So they hurried off and found Mary and Joseph and saw the baby lying in the manger.

It is the middle of summer and I'm sitting writing this outside a motel in Beverly Hills, waiting to be picked up for our first concert in America. Today we lunched in Santa Monica Boulevard and went shopping in Universal City. How's that for cool!

Actually I'm extremely hot, shockingly tired, unbelievably nervous, and a bit defeated. I can't find a hairbrush, we've lost all the postcards we've been carrying around for a week and I've got several bulging bags of dirty washing and no laundry facilities! Moreover my internal clock is completely up the creek as we travelled from New Zealand yesterday leaving at eleven in the evening and arriving at three in the afternoon on the same day. Oh, and I'd do anything for a nice cup of English tea! Reality is very messy isn't it?

For the first time in my life I've had the chance to watch the American Christian Television channel. I've heard how weight loss, jobs, money, influence and power can all be mine if I just say yes to Jesus. I've had verses supporting this from just about every book in the Bible and all it needs is a titsy-witsy gift of money. So many words, so many promises. It feels increasingly like the sort of car advert you find in glossy magazines and reminds me of the junk mail that showers though our letter box promising amazing offers on everything from double glazing to coffins, along with the 'personalized' computer-based nonsenses informing us that we have won £50,000 (in large print) on the outsize envelope and inside telling us (in extremely small print) that this means we could be included in a draw along with a million other lucky people—if we reply within a day agreeing to more bumf being sent.

Mary stands as an example of the unreality of all this. As Adrian once wrote, God appears to have reacted in a somewhat bizarre way to the birth of Jesus, blowing the budget on angel effects to the point that he couldn't afford bed and breakfast for the chosen mother of his Son.

Her lifestyle has not been enhanced one jot by her acceptance of the job God offered her. There were no special perks, no freebies, no bonuses and no long-term security offered. The same somewhat unusual job prospects applied to John the Baptist, the disciples, Paul and indeed still today to those of us who have said yes to the chance of being an employee in God's firm.

Reality is very different from fairy tales. Very messy.

Just a thought. If Jesus had been born in the inn, surrounded by cooing relatives, I doubt if the shepherds would have dared to go in and see him, especially in their work clothes. The messy vulnerability set the pattern of extraordinary accessibility that distinguished the life of Jesus and is a mark of his closest followers.

But then the Gospels are not fairy tales!

PRAYER

Dear Father,

Thank you for reminding us that what you have always offered us is not what the world offers. Help us to distinguish between what we greedily want for ourselves and the things we really need to bring us closer to you. Help us to remain open to anything and anyone that you want to bring into our lives. Please use us in your service. Amen.

AVOID SPILLAGE!

LUKE 2:25−33, 41−43, 46−49, 51

At that time there was a man named Simeon living in Jerusalem. He was a good, God-fearing man and was waiting for Israel to be saved. The Holy Spirit was with him and had assured him that he would not die before he had seen the Lord's promised Messiah. Led by the Spirit, Simeon went into the Temple. When the parents brought the child Jesus into the Temple to do for him what the Law required Simeon took the child in his arms and gave thanks to God:

'Now, Lord you have kept your promise,
and you may let your servant go in peace.
With my own eyes I have seen your salvation,
which you have prepared in the presence of all peoples:
A light to reveal your will to the Gentiles
and bring glory to your people Israel.'

The child's father and mother were amazed at the things Simeon said about him...

Every year the parents of Jesus went to Jerusalem for the Passover Festival. When Jesus was twelve years old, they went to the festival as usual. When the festival was over they started back home, but the boy Jesus stayed in Jerusalem.

On the third day his parents found him in the Temple, sitting with the Jewish teachers listening to them and asking questions. All who heard him were amazed at his intelligent answers. His parents were astonished when *they saw him and his mother said to him, 'My son, why have you done this to us? Your father and I have been terribly worried trying to find you.' He answered them, 'Why did you look for me? Didn't you know that I had to be in my Father's house?'... His mother treasured all these things in her heart.*

In the early years of our marriage Adrian was completing his long-interrupted education and had returned to college to train as a teacher—and he was way behind with a vital assignment.

'Let me help,' I pleaded. 'You dictate—I'll write.' What an idyllic little picture of wedded bliss this conjures up doesn't it? Forget it! For hours I sat pen in hand watching with increasing frustration as he stalked up and down our tiny living-room, flicking channels on the TV, making and drinking coffee and producing not a word. Just at the point when I was about to throw down the pen and go grumpily to bed he said, 'Right, here we go.' He then dictated a 2,000-word essay without stopping. The whole thing was written in his head, including every comma and full stop. A process of slow percolation had taken place and the brew was full of flavour with not a drop spilled.

Many years later I was reminded of that evening. For a few months after Adrian experienced his crack-up he underwent analysis counselling until the stress involved in paying for it outweighed its usefulness! This period proved a great strain for me, because his counsellor insisted that he must not share any of his thoughts or feelings with me but save them up for her. She called the process 'avoiding spillage'.

Difficult as it was for both of us I could see her point even then. It would have been so easy to dilute the potency by adding cupfuls of weak wisdom, and 'similar' memories, while tea-spoons of comfort intended to sweeten the acrid flavour of the most bitter memories might have made the time more palatable for us but could have disguised the poison and made it more difficult for the counsellor to detect.

Now I see the same thing happening again in a different way. 'That can't possibly work', 'I just don't see it', 'They'll never buy it' are phrases that can greet a new idea Adrian shares in its undercooked state and cause him to doubt its potential. Now he just avoids spillage!

Mary seems instinctively to have understood the value of avoiding spillage. Holding each new insight within her and allowing them to blend together and marinade slowly over a period of years must have created a rare maturity and depth of understanding concerning her son's mission to us. She was going to need every drop of understanding to cope with the three years which would constitute his life's work here.

She was going to have to let him go and share him in a way few mothers have ever been called to do. There were going to be times when feeding on these memories of these early prophecies and incidents would have been all she had to reassure her that he was in fact God.

It occurs to me that some of the times when we are blessed with a tiny glimpse of the kingdom, whether through a word or a feeling, we might be wise to 'treasure it in our hearts' for a while. To allow it to percolate our system, seeing the experience as one herb in a bouquet garni, intended to subtly and slowly add flavour to our lives rather than represent a feast.

To share it immediately can subject it to a scrutiny than was not intended, and to a superficial or slighting interpretation. To hold it close and add it to everything else happening during a particular period of time may help to form a clearer and deeper picture of what God is trying to communicate to us.

Dear Father,

We know there are times when it is right to share immediately the things we think you are saying to us. There are other times when it seems important to hold them close, to let them grow, to treat them as just part of the overall pattern that you are developing in our understanding. Help us to discern what we should do with the things you say to us so that where necessary we can avoid spillage and in doing so grow in our trust in you. Amen.

NEVER THE SAME AGAIN

JOHN 2:1−5, 7−10

There was a wedding in the town of Cana in Galilee. Jesus' mother was there, and Jesus and his disciples had also been invited to the wedding. When the wine had given out, Jesus' mother said to him, 'They have no wine left.'

'You must not tell me what to do,' Jesus replied, 'My time has not yet come.'

Jesus' mother then told the servants, 'Do whatever he tells you.'... Jesus said to the servants, 'Fill these jars with water.' They filled them to the brim, and then he told them, 'Now draw some water out and take it to the man in charge of the feast.' They took him the water, which now had turned into wine, and he tasted it... and said to the bridegroom, 'Everyone else serves the best wine first, and after the guests have had plenty to drink, he serves the ordinary wine. But you have kept the best wine until last.'

MARK 3:20−22, 31−33

Then Jesus went home. Again such a large crowd gathered that Jesus and his disciples had no time to eat. When his family heard about it, they set out to take charge of him, because people were saying, 'He's gone mad!'

Then Jesus' mother and brothers arrived. They stood outside the house and sent in a message, asking for him. A crowd was sitting round Jesus and they said to him, 'Look,

your mother and your brothers and sisters are outside,
and they want you.'
  Jesus answered, 'Who is my mother? Who are my
brothers?'

What an amazing contrast there is between these two stories—a period of radical change both in the nature of Jesus' ministry and in his mother's reaction.

At Cana we see Mary in control, sure of her ground, confident in her relationship with Jesus. I love the exchange: 'My time has not yet come'—'Do whatever he tells you'!

How proud she must have felt. How much she must have looked forward to the years to come, anticipated the fulfilment of prophecies she has been hugging to herself for so many years.

A matter of months later everything has changed. The sparkling trickle of living water sufficient to change water into wine has become a raging torrent, smashing through anything growing in its path, unseating established boulders of rules and traditions, rushing into uncharted areas of thought and relationship, swilling out dirt and darkness and ignorance. There is a wildness in this relentless flood and for Mary it must have been shocking and frightening, apparently totally out of control.

Here instead of being respected as a king he was being accused of being mad and even evil. His brothers are clearly ashamed and anxious, going off to fetch their mum to sort him out. We don't know how she felt, struggling through the crowds. Forced to send a message to her son via the jostling queue, asking strangers to tell him to come out and have a word with her.

We can only imagine the shock she must have felt at his reply—the bewilderment, possibly even humiliation. Why did it have to be like that? Maybe it was the only way to break the pattern. To force her to face the truth, to accept his separateness both as her adult son and as her Saviour. What we do know is that her world and indeed the world we have inherited was never to be the same again.

We all have preconceived ideas of how God will do things. We plan our missions, our futures, our families. We know what we would do if we were God, how we would go about things. Nothing prepares us for the times in our lives when the spiritual floods come. Familiar landmarks are in danger of being swept away and the landscape suddenly becomes unfamiliar and frightening.

At these times we always have two choices with God. We can retreat to the banks, climb up onto dry ground and remain safe but lonely. Or we can plunge into the raging waters of the Spirit and allow ourselves to be swept along in the biggest, scariest adventure we have ever had.

The living waters will unearth stubborn boulders of doubt, prejudice and sin, will churn up the mud covering buried memories, and will cleanse and purify to an extent undreamt of. They will take us into areas we never expected to go at a speed we never meant to travel.

Mary had this choice. I have it. So do you.

The only thing I am sure about is that if I choose that way, in the words of a Geoff Bullock song, 'I will never be the same again.'

PRAYER

Dear Father,

Help us to open our hearts to whatever you want of us, whatever the cost. To open our lives so that you can use us, however you want. Help us to choose your way, the way of the unexpected. Help us to let go of the banks and allow ourselves to be swirled along in the frothing living waters of the Holy Spirit trusting in his direction and in his power. Amen.

No Fairy-Tale Ending

Acts 1:12−14; 2:1−4

Then the apostles went back to Jerusalem from the Mount of Olives, which is about a kilometre away from the city. They entered the city and went up to the room where they were staying: Peter, John, James and Andrew, Philip and Thomas, Bartholomew and Matthew, James son of Alphaeus, Simon the Patriot, and Judas son of James. They gathered there to pray as a group, together with the women and with Mary, mother of Jesus and with his brothers...

When the day of Pentecost came all the believers were gathered together in one place. Suddenly there was a noise from the sky which sounded like a strong wind blowing, and it filled the whole house where they were sitting. Then they saw what looked like tongues of fire which spread out and touched each person there. They were all filled with the Holy Spirit and began to talk in other languages as the Spirit enabled them to speak.

Leaping ahead past all the Easter events, here Mary is again! This is the wonderful dénouement of the story as far as she is concerned. She has seen it through from beginning to end, or perhaps I should say to a new beginning! Her son has become her Lord. She is now no longer primarily a mother. She is first and foremost a disciple.

So what can we learn from her? Essentially the value of staying stuck in, of resilience, of loyalty. I can't help feeling that we, the Church, have become rather a greedy bunch. Or at any rate, some of us have. Like fat little baby birds we want spiritual experience and we want it *now*! If we don't get it we will, in the immortal words of Violet Elizabeth Bott, 'scream and scream until we're sick'. We expect to be allocated a selection of the gifts of the Spirit in a kitbag as soon as we join the ranks of the disciples.

We express our boredom if the church we are in is slow to deliver the goods. We moan if the sermon didn't hold our attention or if the worship was a bit below par. We change churches if the going gets tough. Please don't think I'm criticizing you. I'm using myself as a reference point. I've been there, done that! I've sought for perfection and felt fed up when life appears to have let me down.

Take last Easter, for example. We had been hoping to give the children who attend our Saturday club a little glimpse of why Easter was so special. I was helping a rather motley crew of children make gardens. If you didn't look at the huge pile of mud and chaos outside and only looked at the lines of foil containers, each containing grassy mounds, tiny wooden crosses made from split lolly sticks, and an assortment of flowers, then you, like me, would have been enchanted.

They were justifiably proud of their work and I felt we had managed to create something of the wonder and perfection of Easter morning for them. We sat in a circle for our story about the resurrection and while I was telling it I couldn't help feeling a little smug.

Suddenly I heard a yell and looking up saw two of my little gardeners engaged in something far removed from the peaceful atmosphere I had hoped to create. Locked in combat, snarling and yelping they were slugging it out to the death over by the Easter garden table.

Abandoning Mary Magdalene to the mystery of 'Who was that disguised gardener?' I rushed over and attempted to prise them apart. Not easy, as clearly one of the most effective strategies they had learnt in the school of life was holding on to large tufts of hair and pulling hard. Eventually they stood before me gasping for breath, tears furrowing the layers of garden mud on their faces.

Jamie was first to explode indignantly. 'S'not fair, Miss. 'E pinched my snail!'

'He did what?' As a reason for a duel it had to be one of the strangest!

'I had a snail, Miss, in me garden. 'E's pinched it. Look, it's in 'is garden now.'

I looked. Sure enough, Jamie's garden was snailless and a small snail reposed in the adjacent foil container. Irrefutable evidence. But even Watson might have noticed the fine line of silvery slime crossing the path between the foil rims.

'Was the snail dead, Jamie?'

'No, Miss.'

'I think he may have walked on to Clive's garden, Jamie.'

'Yeah... mine's better than yours, that's why,' sneered a relieved Clive.

Before Jamie felt forced to justify with his fists the merits of his garden I dragged both of them to the circle and somehow carried on with the story. The morning had lost its glow! But Mary would have understood. She knew about reality. She had simply lived her life doing what she thought was right at each stage of the way.

Some of it had been frightening, some wonderful, some scary, some amazing, some humdrum and some appalling. She never quit even when the going got horrible, and here she was at the beginning of yet another chapter. We don't know what happened to her after this. We don't hear of her again but I would be very surprised if she didn't continue to lend her support and loyalty to the acts of the disciples. She's just that sort of person.

One thing's for sure: her life hadn't been a fairy tale and this isn't a neat ending. Life just isn't like that. The new churches would have their problems, the disciples would have their differences, she would have her highs and lows. The Church always has and always will have and Jesus never promised joy without pain.

But if there are people like Mary around there will always be the potential for new beginnings and continued growth, because there will always be someone around prepared to serve, prepared to say 'yes' to life, and if that means wonderful presents from the Holy Spirit, then all the better.

PRAYER

Dear Father,

Thank you so much for Mary. Help us to be more like her. Amen.

SECTION 4

SOME FAMOUS LAST WORDS

As Jesus approached his death he seems to have felt able to talk more directly to his followers about the things close to his heart. The images are less obscure, the implications of his stories more carefully explained. There is only time here to look at a few of them, but I think that even this small selection reflects the positiveness of the message of Jesus. By that I don't mean the power of positive thinking. I mean the deep inner confidence of knowing that one is loved and valued through and through by a Father who is crackers about his children.

LEAN BACK AND RELAX

JOHN 15:1–9 (NIV)

I am the true vine. and my Father is the gardener. He cuts off every branch in me that bears no fruit, while every branch that does bear fruit he trims clean so that it will be even more fruitful. You are already clean because of the word that I have spoken to you. Remain in me, and I will remain in you. No branch can bear fruit by itself; it must remain in the vine. Neither can you bear fruit unless you remain in me.

I am the vine; you are the branches. If a man remains in me and I in him, he will bear much fruit; apart from me you can do nothing. If anyone does not remain in me, he is like a branch that is thrown away and withers; such branches are picked up, thrown into the fire and burned. If you remain in me and my words remain in you, ask whatever you wish, and it will be given you. This is my Father's glory, that you bear much fruit, showing yourselves to be my disciples.

As the Father has loved me, so have I loved you. Now remain in my love.

'Mum, we've been having a lot of serious discussion and we all feel that it's now or never for our band, so I don't think I'll be going back to university next year.' Silence falls. The air thickens with tension. My nineteen-year-old son and I look at each other. What do I say? What the heck do I say? Help! (Where's Adrian?!) Definitely a 'lean-back situation'.

I'll explain. Many years ago, during his early years in childcare, Adrian learnt one of the fundamental rules in dealing with an aggressive or threatening situation. Never leave the safety of your position and enter the fight on their ground. Always lean back, try to look relaxed, make yourself talk calmly, and pray! Now I'm not pretending that we've managed to do that too often during our own children's teenage years, but I do know that when we have managed it has helped to diffuse many a tense situation.

This was definitely such an occasion. Everything in me wanted to scream at him: 'What about your future? Don't you care? How can you be so stupid? What about all the sacrifices...?' and so on! I leant back, pressing my back against the cushions of the sofa. 'That sounds interesting...'

Lean back. It is this way of behaving that accounts for why this image means so much to me. 'I am the vine and you are the branches... Remain in me... Apart from me you can do nothing.'

Whenever I get in a situation where I feel out of my depth (and being me that happens all the time) I try to remember these words. I imagine the Father standing behind me, strong, loving and all-wise and I lean back on him in my mind, my arms entwined with his. I feel his strength and sometimes even his wisdom and insight ease into me and I relax, secure in the knowledge that I am, in some way that I will never fully understand, plugged into his bloodline, the sap of the vine. I take such comfort in the fact that I am one of his branches. A branch that has often been buffeted so hard that it has nearly snapped, but nevertheless, one that remains attached.

Have you ever wondered where the expression 'sapping of strength' came from? I don't actually know myself but I do know that when I rush into situations that are very difficult and try to cope on my own I quickly use up my very limited resources. When I acknowledge my dependence on my spiritual Father and remember to lean back, allowing the sap of the Holy Spirit to flow through me, I am refreshed and strengthened, and sometimes even bear an grape or two.

Dear Father,

When the going gets tough—for whatever reason—
help us to lean back and revel in our closeness and
family attachment to you. Fill us with the sap of
your loving kindness so that our work for you
doesn't get dried up and withered.

WALK IN THE LIGHT

JOHN 12:31 – 36 (NIV)

*Jesus said, 'Now is the time for judgment on this world;
now the prince of this world will be driven out. But I,
when I am lifted up from the earth, will draw all men to
myself.' He said this to show the kind of death he was
going to die.*

*The crowd spoke up, 'We have heard from the Law that
the Christ will remain forever, so how can you say, "The
Son of Man must be lifted up"? Who is this Son of Man?'*

*Then Jesus told them, 'You are going to have the light
just a little while longer. Walk while you have the light,
before darkness overtakes you. The man who walks in the
dark does not know where he is going. Put your trust in
the light while you have it, so that you may become sons of
light.' When he had finished speaking, Jesus went and hid
himself from them.*

For months I followed the same carefully thought-out plan.
Every single night the same pattern. First sliding my cramped
fingers free from their manacles and then, without taking a
breath, uncurling from my crouched position on the floor and
rising cautiously to my feet.

Everything from then on depended on my intimate knowledge
of my surroundings as I moved slowly backwards, taking infinite
care not to come in contact with the many obstacles I knew
existed in the darkness behind me. The minutest sound, the tiniest
squeak and all would be lost. I had learnt to squeeze silently

through the crack of the door which I had surreptitiously opened earlier in readiness for my escape.

Then, heart thumping, I would wait for signs of stirring from the occupant of the room I had just left, knowing that recapture was all too possible. At last, breathing more easily, I would head for freedom.

Before you begin to believe that I am some unsung heroine involved in wildly heroic undercover war work I'll explain. The occupant of the room whose waking could have proved so disastrous was our two-year-old son Matthew, notorious among family and babysitters alike for his inability to fall asleep without holding his mummy or daddy's hand.

At the time we felt very ashamed of the ridiculous lifestyle this need inflicted on us. We were sure that we were the only couple in the world who took it in turns to crouch for hours in the dark, singing endless nursery rhymes and even simulating the heavy breathing of sleep until, yawning, miserable and cramped, eventually our patience might be rewarded by the heavenly sounds of sleep-induced huffings and snufflings. (It was one of our best moments when we met a couple in Birmingham who confessed that their small daughter wouldn't succumb unless she had both parents lying beside her!)

We've since met many young parents who have suffered in this way and the one thing we have all agreed on is that the key to successful escape lay in familiarity with the terrain gained during daylight hours! Of course intimate knowledge of one's immediate surroundings can be used to much more purpose in the preparation of those facing long-term blindness, and it is seen as the key to unlocking independence and freedom for many.

Independence and freedom. That is exactly what Jesus is trying to prepare his friends for, a time when they will have to hack it on their own. In these final days we see him again and again pointing them forward while encouraging them to gather all they can from the present. And as they look at him, what do they see?

No long-dreamt-of trips to the equivalent of Florida, no settling of scores. Just the same consistent care for them they had always seen. The same constant safe light that had steered them clear of so many rocks during the last three years. And he is asking them to be the same. Sons of light.

Recently a lovely member of our church was hurled into darkness.

Her husband, Colin, arrived home from work one day with severe earache. By next morning he had been rushed unconscious to hospital and died a week later, never having fully regained consciousness.

As we gathered like stricken sheep in church on Sunday, the day after his death, our vicar gave us this message from our friend. She said, 'I just want to tell you that I'm all right and Colin is very all right.' Well, of course, she wasn't—and her grieving will be part of her for ever. But we as a congregation were moved to the depths of our being that in the midst of her worst hour she had thought of those worrying about her. She said afterwards, 'I was so anxious that this might cause some to stumble.'

Edna's reflection of the light had become a part of her, and quite naturally illumined the path of those stumbling after her.

PRAYER

Dear Father,

Help those of us who are not at present in darkness to appreciate to the full the joy of being with you in the light. Help us to absorb the light of your teaching so that however dark our surroundings become we will always have the comfort of your candle of hope and love and the ability to be a light to illumine the path of your little ones.

CHECK YOUR YEAST!

MATTHEW 13:33–34 (NIV)

The kingdom of heaven is like yeast that a woman took and mixed into a large amount of flour until it worked all through the dough.

MATTHEW 16:5–9, 11–12 (NIV)

When they went across the lake the disciples forgot to take any bread. 'Be careful,' Jesus said to them. 'Be on your guard against the yeast of the Pharisees and Sadducees.'

They discussed this among themselves and said, 'It is because we didn't bring any bread.'

Aware of their discussion, Jesus asked, 'You of little faith, why are you talking among yourselves about having no bread? Do you still not understand? Don't you remember the five loaves for the five thousand, and how many basketfuls you gathered? How is it you don't understand that I was not talking to you about bread? But be on your guard against the yeast of the Pharisees and Sadducees.' Then they understood that he was not telling them to guard against the yeast used in bread, but against the teaching of the Pharisees and Sadducees.

I'm about to show my age and discover yours! Do you remember ginger-beer plants? This usually serves to separate the sheep among us from the lambs! They were a wonderful and almost mystical part of my summers when I was small. A mixture of ginger and yeast formed the base of the concoction. After it had doubled in size you divided it in two and could give half away to someone else to begin their own cottage industry.

I can remember the pride I felt watching my mother place a lump of the smelly dark wet sand that was the ginger-beer plant into a jam jar to give to a neighbour. And I can remember the questions in my mind. How could it be a plant at all when I knew jolly well that plants had green leaves and grew in earth in the garden? How did it grow? How could something so horrid-looking produce such lovely drink? Where did the bubbles come from, for goodness sake?

The ginger beer itself always seemed so special! I can see the bottles now with their glass stoppers standing on the cool stone flags of the pantry—and can hear the awful explosion of a bottle that wasn't properly secured.

Do you realize I am talking pre-Coca-Cola days here? My children can't believe how we survived such tragic times! This Coke deprivation in childhood does mean that I have a particular love for the very name 'yeast' and it is my favourite picture from the many that Jesus uses to describe the kingdom of heaven. (I don't have similar childhood experiences of mustard seeds, tending to associate them with saucers filled with wet cotton wool growing the stuff you put in egg sandwiches. No birds would ever have been able to perch in those branches!)

Mingled with these memories are those connected with baking bread. Lumps of stretchy dough to be bashed into shape on the kitchen table, then placed in the darkness of the airing cupboard to secretly perform their magic. The tins with their glowing domes and heavenly smell. The tapping on the base to hear the hollow ring that meant the loaves were cooked to perfection. No wonder estate agents tell us to be sure of baking bread when prospective buyers come round! Yes, yeast has always got very good press.

That's why I find this advice from Jesus rather shocking. The idea of bad yeast is nasty. The concept of bread that looks good but is in fact very bad for you frightens the child in me. But what an image to describe the danger of unwholesome teaching. Bad yeast which poisons the staple diet of the children of God, who acknowledge their need for bread in order to grow strong in their faith.

Teaching like that of the 'sinful Messiah', David Koresh which led his followers to their tragic suicide. Teaching which condoned slavery and apartheid. Teaching which condemns those who do not receive healing as sinners. Teaching which looks good and may even taste good but which is in fact bread of death instead of bread of life.

PRAYER

Dear Father,

We ask for your protection against the Pharisees of today. Help us to sift all teaching through a sieve and check the quality of the yeast involved so that no falsehoods should be allowed to swell in us and so that we shall smell sweet and be wholesome in your sight.

DO FORGET YOUR TOOTHBRUSH?

JOHN 16:5–13, 16–20 (NIV)

'Now I am going to him who sent me, yet none of you asks me, "Where are you going?" Because I have said these things you are filled with grief. But I tell you the truth: It is for your good that I am going away. Unless I go away, the Counsellor will not come to you; but if I go, I will send him to you. When he comes he will convict the world of guilt in regard to sin and righteousness and judgment. In regard to sin because men don't believe in me; in regard to righteousness, because I am going to the Father, where you can see me no longer; and in regard to judgment, because the prince of this world now stands condemned.

'I have much more to say to you, more than you can now bear, but when he, the Spirit of truth comes, he will guide you into all truth...

'In a little while you will see me no more and then after a little while you will see me.'

Some of his disciples said to one another, 'What does he mean by saying, "In a little while you will see me no more and then after a little while you will see me"?'... Jesus saw that they wanted to ask him about this so he said to them, 'Are you asking one another what I meant?... I tell you the truth, you will weep and mourn while the world rejoices. You will grieve but your grief will turn to joy...'

119

How can a tadpole know what it's like to be a frog? What it's like to hop and croak, sun itself on a rock and catch flies with its tongue? Presumably if asked the tadpole would opt for continued life as a tadpole and debate the advantages of pond-dwelling vigorously. How could the disciples understand that something even more exciting than their nomadic life with Jesus was possible? Of course, it was frightening to contemplate.

We were recently privileged while in Australia to speak at a weekend conference for an organization called Crossroads. The organization is committed to improving the quality of life of many physically and mentally disabled adults by offering them adventure and inclusion in all aspects of life. They have taken group members all round the world, facing difficulties head-on, surmounting the insurmountable, giving dignity and greatly helping self-confidence.

The conference was celebrating twenty years of existence and many of the delegates were extremely challenged either physically or mentally. For some it was their first time away from the firm, loving structure of home. Away from rules which had been their route to the small level of independence they had achieved so far. Being able to wash and dress and look after simple matters of hygiene had been hard to learn for some of them, involving firm continuous reinforcement over a long period of time.

Being away from home meant putting into practice their learnt skills—but a bewilderingly new routine made it difficult to stick rigidly to what they had learnt. Hence the following conversation overheard by a friend of ours during our after-breakfast talk.

'It's too long.'

'What's too long?'

'This talk. It's too long.'

'S'not. S'good.'

'No, it's too long. Look, look at my teeth, they're going rotten, see? See! Look at them! They'll all fall out. They're falling out. See? See?'

Clutching his toothbrush, his face was riddled with fear and panic as he frantically stabbed his finger at tooth after tooth. He was near to tears.

How frightened he must have been. Clearly he had been taught that it was essential to clean his teeth immediately after every meal or else they would go rotten and fall out. Oh, he knew the score all right. He hadn't—and they would!

This new transitional phase in his progress towards a life which would offer him adventure as yet undreamt of was confusing and a bit lonely and scary, but clearly essential. His respect for what he had learnt so far would not disappear because he was learning that rules can sometimes be broken, but hopefully he would discover that, while good habits are essential, real security is found in relationships rather than rules.

Next stop for him? The London Underground? Big Ben? The Eiffel Tower?

For the disciples? The releasing of the Holy Spirit, the discovery that Jesus dwelt so deeply in their hearts that he would never leave them—and a ministry of healing and teaching and church planting as yet undreamt of.

For us? It will vary for each one of us but if we do want to be part of the adventure God has specifically planned for us it might be useful to think today, what is the toothbrush we are clutching? Where does our security lie? What principles and traditions are binding us?

The teaching of the toothbrush had not been wrong in itself. But it wasn't the whole truth, and at this stage in our delegate's life it needed to be re-looked at and explained in more detail.

What needs to be re-looked at in our lives in order for us to be able to move on towards a life of greater spiritual independence?

Whatever it is, we—like Jesus' disciples—will need convincing that the truth as we know it is not the whole truth.

PRAYER

Dear Father,

Open our hearts and minds to the truth, the whole truth and nothing but the truth. Help us to become aware today of those things which we need to look at afresh and learn more about in order to move on in our life's adventure. Please don't let our fears and our self-made rules get in the way. Teach us the next step towards independent Jesus-living, so that increasingly we can live securely in you and you in us. Amen.

REAL QUALITY CONTROL

JOHN 17:6–12 (NIV)

'I have revealed you to those whom you gave me out of the world. They were yours; you gave them to me and they have obeyed your word. Now they know that everything you have given me comes from you. For I gave them the words you gave me and they accepted them. They knew with certainty that I came from you, and they believed that you sent me. I pray for them. I am not praying for the world but for those you have given me, for they are yours. All I have is yours, and all you have is mine. And glory has come to me through them. I will remain in the world no longer, but they are still in the world and I am coming to you. Holy Father, protect them by the power of your name—the name you gave me—so that they may be one as we are one. While I was with them I protected them and kept them safe by that name you gave me.'

Recently we had coffee with some friends who help run a community church in a nearby town. They were pretty devastated by a meeting they had had with the leaders of a huge charismatic church which had recently been planted nearby.

I listened to some of the opinions they were voicing and felt the whole argument seemed familiar.

'The thing is,' one of our friends said, 'he compared our roles as like the difference between the hypermarket outside town and the corner shop. He said that they were planning to bus people in from nearby towns and that he saw their role as supplying a huge variety of whatever people needed to stock up with spiritually. What does that say about us? I just don't see how we can compete. Who will still want to come to us when they can get really lively worship, and famous visiting speakers just down the road?'

Of course! That was exactly where I'd heard the arguments before. At a protest meeting held by shopkeepers in our small market town when one of the supermarket giants was proposing to build a branch on the outskirts.

It will draw all the trade from the town centre and more shops will die... It will remove all the life, colour and atmosphere and make what we do have in the town seem dull... We can't compete with their displays... variety... prices... What about all the old, sick and poor who don't have transport and can't make the journey?

The same arguments! The same perhaps well-grounded fears.

So what happens if we examine the argument in the light of our friends' situation?

There are some wonderful big churches around, with exciting worship bands, imaginative children's work, dynamic youth groups, excellent preaching and confident opportunities to receive the Holy Spirit. They are as much fun to visit as the huge exciting supermarket. There are all sorts of good reasons for attending such a church, and fears and prejudices are often unjustified.

But there are dangers. There is sometimes insensitivity to the long-term effects of their presence on the local community. Sometimes life is drawn out of the local churches and there is little encouragement to those who leave their local churches to remain involved at a local level. This can leave the local church feeling hurt and deskilled.

Then there is 'quality' as Jesus would have meant it. In both types of 'supermarket' the quality and variety of goods is excellent and its packaging very attractive. But at what cost? Where are the irregular-shaped apples and knobbly carrots? Anyone who has ever done a stint in a supermarket knows the answer. They are rejected automatically because they sully the perfect look.

There are some churches where the same thing happens, where those whose emotional shape has been deformed by encounters with stones while growing up are rejected and made to feel less worthy than those whose outward appearance is more acceptable.

This represents a serious waste of resources and, as far as the church is concerned, can be appallingly cruel. The only thing I would say is that many glossy apples I have bought are soft and powdery inside and home-grown knobbly carrots have the best flavour!

Then there is the fact that there is nowhere more impersonal than a supermarket with its mindless and endless music. The supermarket is not where I run in an emergency. It's not where I bump into people I know. It's not where I know the manager and share in his or her life in any way. It's not 'mine' in any way and doesn't need my input. Can this in any way be applied to the church situation?

Jesus brings 'Those you have given me' to his Father and sets a pattern for church life that the disciples go on to emulate. A safe community where the vulnerable are cared for, where the young can grow and where the needs of each member are of paramount importance to the leaders.

If the huge churches are doing these things then they will be sensitive to the needs of little local churches and see part of their job as offering them support. If the small local churches are doing these things they will see part of their job as praying for and befriending those working in the big churches. They will comfortably recognize what they can gain from coming in contact with lively worship and feel free to encourage their young to get involved. What will not work is suspicion and anger on the one hand and greed and insensitivity on the other.

None of it really matters except that when we get to heaven we will be able to say, 'I have revealed you to those you gave me.' But have we?

Dear Father,

Please show me today those whom you gave me to love and care for. Please forgive me for the times I have forgotten to pray for them and help me to take more responsibility for their relationship with you.

OPEN THE PACKET

JOHN 12:23–30 (NIV)

Jesus replied, 'The hour has come for the Son of Man to be glorified. I tell you the truth, unless a grain of wheat falls to the ground and dies, it remains only a single seed. But if it dies it produces many seeds. The man who loves his life will lose it, while the man who hates his life in this world will keep it for eternal life. Whoever serves me must follow me, and where I am my servant also will be. My Father will honour the one who serves me.

'Now my heart is troubled and what shall I say? "Father, save me from this hour?" No, it was for this very reason I came to this hour. Father, glorify your name!'

Spring when I was a small child meant proudly assisting in the planting of beans. I was Holder-Opener of the packet and Bean Selector. My father was Hole Maker and Planter General. Together over the weeks that followed we were Progress Inspectors! I remember being tremendously impressed by the size of the plant that could grow from this tiny thing and the number of beans he and I could pick from the patch of garden where they were nurtured. The miracle of life which in turn produces life was as powerful an image then as now.

It is in this context of procreation that Jesus sets the idea of dying to self. I find this interesting. Somehow I had always associated the idea of hating one's life with self-denial and even self-destruction. I found it confusing that my creator should want me to hate the life he created. But here we see him suggesting that glory lies in the giving of self. That blessings will multiply and that a new and more vigorous life will flourish, while hugging life to oneself is inevitably sterile. But acknowledging the barrenness of our present situation doesn't always make handing over the control of our lives easy. It seems it has to cost to be worthy of the giving. We have to accept and agree that the hour we have come to is the very one that was planned for us in order that God may be glorified, and that can be hard.

There have been times in my life which I have found very hard. I'm sure there have been in yours. Times which feel as if they cannot possibly be part of what a loving Father can have intended for me as one of his children.

I have learnt that the first thing I have to do at these times is to look clearly at what is happening. I often have to accept the hard fact that the circumstances surrounding me aren't going to change. That it is up to me to stop bashing on the walls of my prison (an exhausting and futile business) and begin to face up to the fact that change of some sort in me is essential if I'm going to be able to adapt to new circumstances.

A friend of ours said recently that she had come to realize that most decisions were between what you don't want and what you *really* don't want. For example, when I was experiencing difficulties with the job God has chosen for Adrian, although I was feeling very unhappy and confused I *really* didn't want to ruin the work God had given Adrian to do. And I *really* didn't want our relationship to be spoiled and I *really* missed my sense of closeness with God. And I *hated* feeling guilty!

At first I tried to change myself. To superimpose acceptance on to my then state of mind by an effort of will while still holding fast to the closed packet of my life. This failed totally and I became increasingly bitter and unhappy.

Eventually I turned back to my Father in heaven, and in an atmosphere of familiar closeness with my Lord I was able at last to open the packet of pain I had been clutching to me. I even managed to take a bean or two and give them to him to be planted. My packet is still half full, I'm afraid. (Maybe heaven is rejoicing that it's half empty!) Still, it's pretty exciting waiting to see what crop will grow from those I *have* been able to entrust to him.

Perhaps for you it will be a cataclysmic crisis that will allow you to give over control of your life. Maybe it has already happened. But if, like me, you are still finding this difficult, remember that the first step is to open the packet!

PRAYER

Dear Father,

Show us how to begin to give you our lives. Be close to us today so that in your presence we can peep at some of the things that are troubling us. Help us to take one bean into our hands today. Help us to stretch out our hands to you and give it to you. Help us to trust you have taken it. Give us courage not to take it back, not to close the packet, so that at last it can be sown and in time produce a useful crop for you. Amen.

A PROMISE OF WELCOME

JOHN 13:36 — 14:7 (NIV)

Simon Peter asked him, 'Lord, where are you going?'

Jesus replied, 'Where I am going, you cannot follow now, but you will follow later...

'Do not let your hearts be troubled. Trust in God, trust also in me. In my Father's house are many rooms; if it were not so I would have told you. I am going there to prepare a place for you. And if I go and prepare a place for you, I will come back and take you to be with me that you also may be where I am. You know the way to the place where I am going.'

Thomas said to him, 'Lord, we don't know where you are going, so how can we know the way?'

Jesus answered, 'I am the way and the truth and the life. No one comes to the Father except through me. If you really knew me you would know my Father as well. From now on, you do know him and have seen him.'

She felt so incredibly exhausted. So tired. Bruised with pain and confusion, desperately alone. And it was so dark, the territory so unfamiliar. She clutched her sadness and fear to her—they were all she had.

She thought of her family. So much anger, so many tears that she had to leave them. It had seemed so unfair to them. Explanations had proved useless. Only her husband had really wished her well and told her not to worry, she'd see him soon.

Well, no turning back now. Ever again. Never to see the

familiar things that had meant so much, the furniture she and her husband had lovingly collected over the years. Never to smell burnt toast, wallflowers, baby's talcum powder. Never to hold, to touch those she'd loved so much. Never to hear the dog barking at the postman or the milk bottles jingling as they were placed on the step, or the children's music blaring from behind their closed doors. Imagine, she was even missing that now!

So alone.

A stranger's voice calling her name. Calm and real and somehow familiar. Where was it coming from? Who...?

She began to run, the strength flooding into muscles that she had thought were wasted. The air smelt of spring and sea and baking and home. Dawn was coming, birds waking.

And there he was, standing, waiting. Arms wide, waiting for her—for *her*.

Now she was running, laughing, crying—flinging herself into the safety of his arms.

Everything was going to be all right. She was home at last.

And Jesus, his arm round the most recently arrived member of his family, strolled with her into heaven to introduce her proudly to the Father she had never met but would recognize immediately.

That's the promise. A promise of a room prepared. A promise of welcome. A promise of a Father whom we will recognize because we have met his Son.

But it's also a promise that Jesus will have taken the same route. The same step into darkness. The same prayers to take away the necessity for the journey. The same aloneness. He has already marked the path, trodden down the brambles. He is the Way. If we follow the path he has directed us onto he will meet us and accompany us into heaven.

What a promise!

Lord, this is the hardest journey.

Give those who are now travelling that way the reassurance of your presence beside them at every step. And help the rest of us, in our anger and our tears. Amen.

SECTION 5

'GOD SO LOVED THE WORLD...'

We have reached the point where we are following Jesus to his death. My prayer for all of us is that we hold the hand of the Father as we remember all Jesus went through for us. I suggest this partly because we need his support but also because it is a very special chance for us to allow into our minds the concept of a vulnerable father, grieving for his son yet helpless through his own love for us to intervene in the inevitable horrific course of events.

THE CHOICE IS OURS

JOHN 15:12−15 (NIV)

My command is this: Love each other as I have loved you. Greater love has no one than this, that one lay down his life for his friends. You are my friends if you do what I command. I no longer call you servants because a servant does not know his master's business. Instead, I have called you friends, for everything that I have learned from my father I have made known to you.

We are coming into the long, dark shadow of the cross. From the moment Jesus entered Jerusalem we know his destiny is set. He has chosen. He has said 'yes' to the hardest request ever to be asked of anyone. He himself has chosen to demonstrate that the greatest thing we can do is to lay down our lives for our friends.

We are not going to join those who arrived at the foot of the cross once it was tidily standing on the hill. It is so easy for us to skip over this ghastly chapter in the life of Jesus. Some churches even encourage us to do so, feeling that we should now concentrate on the happy ending. To skip to the last chapter of any book, especially one with a horrifying or tense plot, might be safe or cosy but will mean little to us.

We need to enter fully into the living hell of that terrible week. We need to ban from our minds for a while all images of the glorious risen Lord. This is no actor playing a part who will, at the end of a working day, return to his flat for crumpets and hot chocolate. These are the last days in the life of a man. Of course we know he was also God, but he has chosen to be as powerless and as despairing as any of us would have been.

Do we have the courage to walk with him? It doesn't seem much to ask of ourselves, considering what he has chosen to do for us. Let's go to join the crowds at the gate of Jerusalem.

MEDITATION

We are walking towards Jerusalem. We are silent, afraid. There is something in the air. A new sense of determination in the silent figure whom we are following. He stops. He looks towards Jerusalem. He says something to those near enough to hear. He appears to be weeping. We have a choice. We can go with him or we can quite simply turn away, go home. Home to where it's safe. Where there are no triumphant glances and whispered confidences passing between the Pharisees, no stench of danger. We can go. Or we can follow. We can be there for the dear familiar person who has brought us so much laughter and joy. Shall we follow? Shall we leave? The choice is ours. After all we are no longer servants. We are his friends.

WANTED: ONE DONKEY

JOHN 12:12−19 (NIV)

The next day the great crowd that had come for the Feast heard that Jesus was on his way to Jerusalem. They took palm branches and went out to meet him, shouting

'Hosanna!'

'Blessed is he who comes in the name of the Lord!'

Jesus found a young donkey and sat upon it, as it is written,

'Do not be afraid,

O daughter of Zion;

see, your king is coming,

seated on a donkey's colt.'

At first his disciples did not understand all this. Only after Jesus was glorified did they realize that these things had been written about him and that they had done these things to him.

Now the crowd that was with him continued to spread the word that he had called Lazarus from the tomb, raising him from the dead. Many people, because they had heard that he had given this miraculous sign, went out to meet him. So the Pharisees said to one another, 'See, this is getting us nowhere. Look how the whole world has gone after him!'

From childhood we are taught that Jesus came to save us. That he had to die to reconcile us to the Father by taking on our sins. Yet it was in life as well as death that he sought to reconcile us, by communicating the truth about the Father in as many ways as he could. In his last few days of freedom we see an urgency unparalleled in the rest of his ministry.

Here, on the day we now call Palm Sunday, we see him using an essential opportunity to the full. He knew there would be hundreds of people in Jerusalem because of the Passover and that news of his recent miracle had reached them. He knew they would be there in their droves to see the miracle-maker for themselves (after all, he always understood our human nature perfectly). He has every intention of using this 'photo opportunity' to the full.

In front of this vast chanting crowd, words without a microphone will be useless. So he chooses a visual aid. No high-tech phenomenon: just a little donkey's colt.

Have you ever, as an adult, sat on a seaside donkey or crushed yourself into a kindergarten chair? Everyone knows without much sociological analysis that you look and feel pretty ridiculous! So why did he do it—apart from giving the learned a cryptic clue as to his identity and giving all who lived after him reassurance that scripture had been fulfilled? The reason has to lie in the words from the relevant passage in Zechariah. 'Do not be afraid, O daughter of Zion. See, your king is coming, seated on a donkey's colt.' Jesus is clearly determined to show himself—and through him the Father—as vulnerable and accessible. So what has gone wrong? Why do we represent him in so many strange ways?

A few years ago I was profoundly affected by a poem I read by Steve Turner called 'How to Hide Jesus'. The gist of the poem was that we had successfully hidden him from the masses not by chaining up Bibles so that people couldn't read them but by the strange dress, language and behaviour of his modern representatives.

Recently we met a woman who had been through an appalling experience. We had been told what had happened and felt very sympathetic.

'Has it been awful?' I asked.

'Well, no,' she said with a bright smile. 'It's been a growing time.'

I later found that she had allowed no one into her pain because she had been brought up by evangelists always to seek opportunities to pass on the good things that God was doing in her life. In her obedient attempt to give God a good reference she had cut herself off from the help that she needed, and she was in danger of falling apart.

My fear is that our ridiculous need to represent Jesus by the success in our own lives—materially and emotionally—actually hides him from those who need him. Suppose I have got myself into a real mess, and I'm not a Christian, and I live next door to a woman who seems to be successful in all those ways. How can I possibly tell her about the mess that I'm in? Surely she couldn't possibly understand: she's got her life so together. Surely the God she worships would have no time for a failure like me. Wouldn't I be more inclined to seek the help of a fellow sinner or a secular professional than to open myself to my Christian neighbour?

But if I knew that however much *you* have fouled up, God still loves you and has never let you go then I might dare to think that maybe he would be the same with me.

Perhaps we need to find ourselves the equivalent of a donkey's colt so that present-day daughters (and sons) of Zion need not be afraid of their king.

Dear Father,

Help me today to look for ways in which I can proclaim your love to those who up till now have only heard the rumours. Help me to be vulnerable in my dealings with those who don't know you yet—so that they can see you in me and not just the badly drawn picture of you that my life portrays. Help me to let those who don't know you have a real role in my life from now on. Amen.

HELP US TO QUESTION

MARK 15:12 — 16 (NIV)

'What shall I do with the one you call the king of the Jews?' Pilate asked them.

'Crucify him,' they shouted.

'Why? What crime has he committed?' asked Pilate.

But they shouted all the louder, 'Crucify him!' Wanting to satisfy the crowd, Pilate released Barabbas to them. He had Jesus flogged and handed him over to be crucified.

The soldiers led Jesus away into the palace (that is, the Praetorium) and called together the whole company of soldiers.

From the moment the judge delivered the sentence 'You will go to the cross' the sequence of following events was prescribed. First, the condemned man was removed from view.

We often sing, 'just a closer walk with you'. If you're anything like me you probably picture meandering down a country lane in the warm afternoon sun picking off heads of corn and listening to the master storyteller. But walking closely with Jesus into that closed courtyard and waiting for the company of soldiers would have been quite simply terrifying.

I wonder what the soldiers saw, if they bothered to look into their captive's face. The man so manly that the non-religious felt they could ask him to come for a pint down at the local? The friend with whom women felt free to be themselves without risk of being misunderstood? The adult so cosy that children rushed to hug him whenever they saw him? The man whose storytelling had been so spellbinding that the temple guards returned to the furious Pharisees without their prisoner? Their only defence—'Never did a man speak as he speaks.'

I don't think they saw any of that. Not just because Jesus had chosen powerlessness, but also because of the effect the death sentence can have on those closely involved. Looking at him they would have seen a person whose identity had been removed, a person with no rights, no choices—an object rather than a human being.

What is so frightening is that however much I may condemn the soldiers for their response, I know that I too have been guilty of accepting sentences placed on individuals without question. Character assassination in the newspapers can result in the death of a promising career, emotional torture, the destruction of relationships—even suicide.

Perhaps there is nothing I can do about that, but what about the times when I allow all the good and true things I know about someone to slip to the very back of my mind in order to enjoy a good gossip? Or the times when I accept an embittered account of an incident without checking the facts?

Jesus did not hold the Roman soldiers responsible for their part in his death. He said, 'Father, forgive them, for they know not what they do.'

PRAYER

Dear Father,

If we had been there we know we might well have lacked the courage needed to stand up for the truth. Help us today to walk with you into that courtyard, to face our fear, to see what yours must have been like. We are truly sorry for the times when we have not questioned sufficiently what we have heard about someone we know, when we have believed the rumour and, even worse, when we have passed it on

to someone else. Whatever we have done to one of your children we have done to Jesus. Forgive us Father. Amen.

INJUSTICE COVERED UP

MARK 15:17–20

They put a purple robe on Jesus, made a crown out of thorny branches, and put it on his head. Then they began to salute him: 'Long live the King of the Jews!' They beat him over the head with a stick, spat on him, fell on their knees, and bowed down to him.

This was the next stage in the sentence of crucifixion. I don't think I'd realized this before. This wasn't something laid on especially for Jesus. This didn't stem from a violent hatred. It was quite simply the soldiers' 'treat time'.

We've seen it before. During the Holocaust, in Cambodia, in Japanese prisoner-of-war camps, in the former Yugoslavia. Doubtless we'll see it again. When given permission to do anything they want and when personal responsibility is removed, people often revert to levels of behaviour that are bestial, subhuman. The veneer of civilization that society boasts of turns out to be very thin indeed.

Is it significant that these were Roman soldiers? Respected, uniformed members of the most successful civilization of the day? It is usually when a country is displaying power most forcibly that it is at its most cruel. Arrogance is very dangerous. It separates us in our minds from other people. It offers us the chance to believe that in our superior state we are no longer accountable. Uniforms can have the same effect. At worst they give the wearer a sense of power which can feel like a licence to abuse those of lesser rank. I'm sure we all have experiences of these mini-Hitlers.

Perhaps this is why Jesus chose to live as he did. The example he set of service hardly condones arrogance. At no time in his life did he set himself apart from his followers in terms of lifestyle, dress or language.

To know that we're accountable to such a God can help to keep us from falling into the trap of indifference to others. No wonder Jesus taught us to pray, 'Lead us not into temptation.' I truly believe that vulnerability is our only safeguard against the temptation of misuse of power, whether in a work situation, at home with the family, or even in a situation like that of the Roman soldiers.

MARK 15:20

When they had finished mocking him, they took off the purple robe and put his own clothes back on him.

How I loathe and detest what happened then. Why? Surely the baying mob or the physical torture of our Saviour were much worse. I hate this more because it stinks of a cover-up. My husband Adrian once met a social worker at an interview who had developed a technique of hitting children with a wet towel in such a way that it left no mark. Presumably he thought Adrian would find the information useful in his work with disturbed children.

Then there is a friend of ours who was sexually abused over a long period, beginning when she was eight years old. Her uncle ensured her silence by threatening that he'd tell her parents she'd led him on. Years later I was to hear her sob, 'It was all my fault.' 'How... how was it your fault?' I asked—and she told me. 'He said so.'

Deeply lodged in this woman's mind is the knowledge of guilt. No adult reasoning can remove those hideous false seeds planted there for her attacker's self-protection and covered over with the soil of secrecy.

When the soldiers replaced Jesus' clothes, covering the jagged, torn flesh of their victim, they were removing the evidence in the same way that we have heard the police removed evidence in the case of the Birmingham Six. The need to cover one's tracks is an admission of guilt and has no place in any viable system of justice. Whatever happened behind the locked doors of a Birmingham police station or in the closed courtyard of the governor's palace is history. But the coldness of purpose involved in the cover-up is as hard for me to forgive as the cowardly promise extorted by the uncle of my friend.

PRAYER

Dear Father,

Help us to hate what you hate and to despise what you despise. Give us courage to speak out against injustice and bullying and to tackle those who in any way cause your little ones to stumble. Teach us how to listen to our consciences more clearly and how to fine-tune our heartstrings so that we become aware of how you feel about what is going on around us, and give us the ability to respond. Amen.

JUST BEING THERE

MARK 15:20

Then they led him out to crucify him.

The third stage. Condemned, beaten, and now the cross is placed across the shoulders and the long walk begins. A showy procession by all accounts. At the head a centurion carrying a placard on which is stated the crime. Then four soldiers and, in the centre, the focus of all attention, the man on his way to death. This one had been beaten with a whip made up of leather thongs embedded with pieces of metal.

When I was about fourteen I went youth hostelling with the Girl Guides. One blazing afternoon I fell asleep on a grassy bank outside the hostel. The sunburn kept me awake all night and next morning I had to shoulder my rucksack and walk seven miles to the next hostel. I will never forget it! My rucksack, heavy with sensible wet-weather clothing and clanking with billycans and all-in-one cutlery sets and other useful gadgets, scoured my back every inch of the way. I thought that was bad enough. But there really is no comparison.

The physical pain of dragging this unwieldy and immensely heavy burden was compounded by other things. The humiliation of being the object of derision and the knowledge literally impressed on him every inch of the way that his death lay ahead. I have never been able to rid myself of the memory of those families in Cambodia's Killing Fields who had first to dig their graves, then stand by them waiting to be shot in the back. Carrying your cross was the same. Not for a second, as you stumbled your way through the streets of the city and finally out of the gates and up the hill, could you be distracted from the reality of what your brief future held.

I don't think our close walk with Jesus is improving, do you?

L U K E   2 3 : 2 7

A large group of people followed him; among them were some women who were weeping and wailing for him.

I know it's a rather feminist view but I can't help thinking 'Thank goodness for the women.' Not that I blame the men. The courage Peter showed in entering that courtyard was enormous. And I don't know a soul who wouldn't have been tempted to deny knowing Jesus when faced with the strong possibility of also being taken prisoner on that confusing and frightening night. The women clearly felt safer. I know that. I'm just so glad they were there, mourning openly for him and making his hideous journey a little less lonely.

Being there usually costs less than picking up the end of someone's cross in terms of time and commitment. But it may cost just as much in terms of bringing judgment upon us. We all like to be part of the crowd. It's safer to agree that so-and-so had it coming to them or to shake our communal head over the way certain people we could mention are bringing up their children.

I know from personal experience what it's like to be the object of community disapproval. There is nothing more difficult for people to understand than the depression and angry despair that accompany any sort of emotional breakdown. I cannot put into words what it meant to me, when Adrian was ill in this way in 1984, to have a small handful of people who, I knew, were there for us. Openly caring, allowing their support for us to be heard, never judging us or telling us what we should do.

Yes, I'm so glad the women were there.

Dear Father,

I can't believe that you love us so much that you allowed Jesus to suffer like this for us. Can we really be worth it? There are people we know who are suffering. Help us to walk with them in their desert for as many blistering miles as it takes. Help us to tend to their blisters, to help carry their burdens. But above all, help us never to minimize the extent of their pain. Amen.

SHARE THE BURDEN

L U K E   2 3 : 2 6

... as they were going, they met a man from Cyrene named Simon who was coming into the city from the country.

Did you ever have a childhood hero? I did. No, not a pop singer or an actor. It was this man, Simon of Cyrene! As a child I went to a Catholic junior school. Some aspects were rather bizarre to my Protestant mind, but I loved the flowery processions that signified saints' days and, of course, the days off that accompanied them!

One regular aspect of my schooling involved visiting the chapel, where the height of daring (I seem to remember) was squeezing the sponge of holy water dry and flipping our wet hands over our friends. Despite this I did develop a deep joy at being there. I loved the colour, the candles and the combination of the heavy perfumes of flowers and incense.

But most of all I loved the stations of the cross. The one that always drew me to it first was Jesus stumbling under the weight of the cross and falling on to his poor knees. At the age of seven I didn't understand much about scourging and sacrifice but I did know all about grazed knees and I knew how much it hurt when you were carrying something heavy and crashed with all your weight on them. I remember touching his knees with my finger and the tears that always threatened as I helplessly imagined the pain. Then I would rush to the next one and there was this man, Simon, helping him to lift the weight.

Do you, like me, find it rather amusing to imagine the reaction of some of these 'minor' biblical characters if they had discovered how famous they were to become? Simon of Cyrene, the hero of a plump little girl in the late twentieth century! What would he have said?

They seized him, put the cross on him and made him carry it behind Jesus.

Poor Simon, up for the Passover jamboree, all the way from Cyrene in Northern Africa. Probably been saving up his 'camel miles' for ages! And now... What a way to spend a holiday. Why him? On and on, through the streets of Jerusalem, past the jeering crowds and finally out of the city gates. Of course, it wasn't lawful to crucify a man within the boundaries of the city, he knew that... On in the searing heat and up the hill Simon stumbled unhappily. What would people think?

Let us for a moment stop and take breath. Do we know anyone who is on the point of falling under the weight of the cross they are carrying alone? Maybe it's illness or depression or a failed relationship or redundancy, even bereavement. Often when we look we find it's someone very close to us. Maybe, like Simon, we feel we have been given no choice in helping to carry that burden. Maybe it has hit someone so close to us that we are automatically involved. Maybe we've been asking 'Why me?' and feeling bitter and resentful.

Or perhaps we have a choice. If so we must think carefully, because each cross will need carrying to the top of the hill. Having shouldered the burden it's no good putting it down five yards later. Nor is it any good hoping it will bring glory. It won't. It's no use, either, rushing from person to person picking up crosses—and then dropping them to rush off and help someone else.

Cross-carrying is never easy but it is Jesus' way, and it is our chance day by day to walk close to him on the road to Calvary.

MEDITATION

Come and join Jesus. Feel the weight of your cross piercing the skin of your shoulders and scoring even deeper into the cuts on your back.

Feel the incredible weight of the wood causing your legs to buckle and tremble.

You stop for a moment, waves of nausea making you sway and stumble on the dusty road. You try to see where you are but the blood and sweat dripping through your matted hair blind you.

You try to hear but the shouting and sound of horses' hooves mean you cannot make out what anyone is saying. You feel as if the end is coming, as though you are going to collapse and die there, on the road. You hear a peculiar rasping noise and it takes a moment or two to realize it is the sound of your own breath.

You are urged forward but stumble and fall to your knees. You feel strangely distant from yourself as though you are watching a stranger suffer.

Blackness seeps into your brain. Suddenly you feel the whole cross tip forward as though it has its own life and then you feel the weight lift. You stand shakily.

Someone who you can't see is helping you to carry your cross. You move forward slowly, no longer alone.

PRAYER

Dear Father,

Some of us are burdened and heavily laden. Come to us, we beg you. Help us to keep going. Give us just enough strength to carry on. Some of us know someone who is carrying a burden that is far too heavy for them to carry alone. Give us the courage to pick it up today. Amen.

A WAY TO HELP

MARK 15:22-25

They took Jesus to a place called Golgotha, which means 'The Place of the Skull.' There they tried to give him wine mixed with a drug called myrrh, but Jesus would not drink it. Then they crucified him and divided his clothes among themselves, throwing dice to see who would get which piece of clothing. It was nine o'clock in the morning when they crucified him.

A lot has been said recently about the immunizing effect that so much tragedy on television has had on our emotions. There is only so much that we can bear before our defence system comes into action to prevent further pain. This usually results in a shutdown of our ability to respond, either in the form of toughened cynicism or a deliberate switching off. For some people their inability to change the circumstances they see causes impotent despair.

So much has been said and written about the death of Jesus that our response can be similarly affected, and as I think about him hanging there I am engulfed by helplessness.

I cannot remove this chapter from his life any more than I, as a little girl staring at those stations of the cross, could kiss his poor knees better.

But maybe Jesus has given us a way to enter his tragedy. If, as Mother Teresa believed, Christ is to be found in every suffering soul, then there lies our chance to plaster those knees, to ease the weight from those bleeding shoulders, and to be there for him at the end.

It is a glorious opportunity. Let us take it.

PRAYER

Dear Father,

Thank you for the many opportunities there are for us to help our suffering world. Help us to find the right way for us to make a difference, and to seize the opportunity at whatever cost to ourselves. Amen.

WHEN HOPE IS GONE

J o h n   1 9 : 2 5 − 2 9 ,   3 8

Standing close to Jesus' cross were his mother, his mother's sister, Mary the wife of Clopas, and Mary Magdalene. Jesus saw his mother and the disciple he loved standing there; so he said to his mother, 'He is your son.'

Then he said to the disciple, 'She is your mother.' From that time the disciple took her to live in his home.

Jesus knew that by now everything had been completed... Then he bowed his head and died...

After this, Joseph who was from the town of Arimathea, asked Pilate if he could take Jesus' body. (Joseph was a follower of Jesus, but in secret, because he was afraid of the Jewish authorities.) Pilate said he could have the body, so Joseph went and took it away.

You were there. Standing with the other women close to the cross. Loyal to the very end. How did you feel? Looking at your dear first-born son hanging there, beaten, bruised, humiliated beyond any level of decency. Did you wonder about the truth of the prophecy you had received? 'He will cause the mighty to fall'? Didn't seem too possible now. Simeon's 'sword' piercing your side was far more accurate.

Did you remember his birth, the shepherds, the kings? His first toddling steps, his first words? Oh Mary, how did you feel? Did you feel you had failed? That if you had been able to stem the rushing tide he would be safe now? Did you chide yourself for not seeing the signs earlier? Did you wish Joseph was by your side to lean on? Did you try to be strong for your dying son or did you weep helplessly in your sister's arms?

How was it having Mary Magdalene there? Were you friends, or did she represent the lifestyle that had brought your son to this appalling end? We will never know. All we know is that you were there, with the women. As Anne from Jane Austen's *Persuasion* says: 'All the privilege I claim for my own sex is that of loving longest when existence or when hope is gone.'

The role of parents through the ages has also been to be there when our children are going through the worst of times. It is often all we can do. When Adrian and I were working with children in care we saw so many with large gaping holes inside them which should have been filled with memories of being loved. That's what we can do for our children during the childhood years. We can make all the mistakes in the world but if we have stuffed them full of love we haven't completely failed.

Then we have to let them go. A painful ripping gesture that we probably never quite come to terms with. We have to stand in the wings of their lives, mouthing our support, sometimes having to swallow our jealousy or our criticism of their performance and of those to whom they have given leading roles in their lives. Then and only then have we earned the right to stand there in the worst times. To be there at the cross. Thank you, Mary. You stand in my eyes for the very best of parenting.

PRAYER

Dear Father,

Thank you for the example of the woman you chose to be the mother of your Son. You certainly knew what you were doing! Help us to learn from her. To learn how to be there for those whom we love, whatever it costs. Amen.

ALIVE FOR EVER AND EVER!

MATTHEW 28:1–10 (NIV)

After the Sabbath, at dawn on the first day of the week, Mary Magdalene and the other Mary went to look at the tomb.

There was a violent earthquake, for an angel of the Lord came down from heaven and, going to the tomb, rolled back the stone and sat on it. His appearance was like lightning, and his clothes were white as snow. The guards were so afraid of him that they shook and became like dead men.

The angel said to the women, 'Do not be afraid, for I know that you are looking for Jesus, who was crucified. He is not here; he has risen, just as he said. Come and see the place where he lay. Then go quickly and tell his disciples: "He has risen from the dead and is going ahead of you into Galilee. There you will see him." Now I have told you.'

So the women hurried away from the tomb, afraid yet filled with joy, and ran to tell his disciples. Suddenly Jesus met them. 'Greetings,' he said. They came to him, clasped his feet and worshipped him. Then Jesus said to them, 'Do not be afraid. Go and tell my brothers to go to Galilee; there they will see me.'

Today is one of the most glorious muddles in the whole of the New Testament. You'd have thought that accounts of this day of all days would have tallied! All the Gospel writers have a different tale, a different emphasis. There are stones rolling back and no stone, there is one angel and two, several different women who either do or do not pass on the good news and a whole lot of disciples who either believe or not!

Surely it would have made sense to stick to one storyline, God? But what it shows is that everyone wanted to be part of it and I'm sure everyone knew someone who knew someone who had been there when—and this is the wonderful truth shared by all of them—when Jesus came back to life. But you know, when we consider this glorious truth, we must see it in its full context. Mary Magdalene will have her precious memories—and I so love Jesus for singling out one of his favourite cracked pots for special attention. Peter and John will have their own stories. Even the Roman soldiers had a tale to tell.

But we are the most fortunate because we have all the accounts. We have the hindsight memories of Peter at the time of Pentecost—and we have the amazing revelation to John that the Jesus that came back is in fact the risen Lord in all his glory.

REVELATION 1:12–18 (NIV)

I turned round to see the voice that was speaking to me. And when I turned I saw seven golden lampstands, and among the lampstands was someone 'like a son of man', dressed in a robe reaching down to his feet and with a golden sash round his chest. His head and hair were white like wool, as white as snow, and his eyes were like a blazing fire. His feet were like bronze glowing in a furnace, and his voice was like the sound of rushing waters. In his right hand he held seven stars, and out of his mouth came a sharp double-edged sword. His face was like the sun shining in all its brilliance.

When I saw him, I fell at his feet as though dead. Then he placed his right hand on me and said: 'Do not be afraid. I am the First and the Last. I am the Living One; I was dead, and behold I am alive for ever and ever! And I hold the keys of death and Hades.'

And to me this is the best truth of all. All-mighty, all-powerful, it is he who stands and knocks at the door of our hearts. He who wants to come into the house of our life and eat with us and we with him. The risen Lord of Glory whose face shines like the sun. The Holy One of God, our creator and our dearest friend.

If you have enjoyed reading *The Apple of His Eye*, you may wish to know that Bridget Plass is a regular contributor to *Day by Day with God*, a series of daily Bible reading notes written by women for women, published jointly by The Bible Reading Fellowship and Christina Press. *Day by Day with God* is published three times a year (in January, May and September) and contains a printed Bible passage for each day, plus a brief comment and a prayer or reflection.

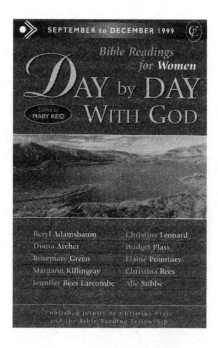

Copies of *Day by Day with God* may be obtained from your local Christian bookshop or by subscription direct from BRF.

A free sample copy of *Day by Day with God* may be obtained by sending an A5 SAE with 36p stamp marked 'Day by Day with God' to BRF.

For more information about the full range of BRF publications, write to: The Bible Reading Fellowship, Peter's Way, Sandy Lane West, Oxford OX4 5HG. Tel: 01865 748227; fax: 01865 773150; e-mail: enquiries@brf.org.uk